READING ALICE MUNRO WITH JACQUES LACAN

ISBN 978-0-7735-4781-0 (cloth)
ISBN 978-0-7735-9984-0 (ePDF)
ISBN 978-0-7735-9985-7 (ePUB)

Legal deposit third quarter 2016
Bibliothèque nationale du Québec

Printed in Canada on acid-free paper that is 100% ancient forest free (100% post-consumer recycled), processed chlorine free

This book has been published with the help of a grant from the Canadian Federation for the Humanities and Social Sciences, through the Awards to Scholarly Publications Program, using funds provided by the Social Sciences and Humanities Research Council of Canada.

McGill-Queen's University Press acknowledges the support of the Canada Council for the Arts for our publishing program. We also acknowledge the financial support of the Government of Canada through the Canada Book Fund for our publishing activities.

Library and Archives Canada Cataloguing in Publication

Murray, Jennifer, 1963–, author
Reading Alice Munro with Jacques Lacan / Jennifer Murray.

Includes bibliographical references and index.
Issued in print and electronic formats.
ISBN 978-0-7735-4781-0 (cloth). – ISBN 978-0-7735-9984-0 (ePDF). –
ISBN 978-0-7735-9985-7 (ePUB)

1. Munro, Alice, 1931– – Criticism and interpretation. 2. Lacan, Jacques, 1901–1981. 3. Psychoanalysis and literature. 4. Desire in literature. 5. Canadian fiction (English) – 20th century – History and criticism. I. Title.

PS8576.U57Z79 2016 C813'.54 C2016-903773-8
C2016-903774-6

This book was typeset by Marquis Interscript in 11.5/14 Garamond.

Reading Alice Munro with Jacques Lacan

JENNIFER MURRAY

McGill-Queen's University Press
Montreal & Kingston · London · Chicago

Contents

Acknowledgments

My first thanks go to the staff at McGill-Queen's University Press, particularly to Mark Abley, who gave me encouragement and constructive advice in the early stages of the editorial process, and to Kathleen Fraser for her friendly and efficient support in the final stretch. I am also grateful to the anonymous readers who welcomed my project and engaged with it in detail, and to Ellie Barton for her rigorous and insightful copy editing.

This book has been published with the help of a grant from the Federation for the Humanities and Social Sciences, through the Awards to Scholarly Publications Program, using funds provided by the Social Sciences and Humanities Research Council of Canada.

Two of the chapters were previously published and are reprinted here in slightly modified form by kind permission of the publishers:

- "'Like the Downflash of a Wing or Knife': Repression, Sublimation, and the Return of the Repressed in Alice Munro's 'Princess Ida,'" *Journal of the Short Story in English* 55 (autumn 2010): 55–69
- "'Not Entirely on His Side': The Assumption of Sexed Subjectivity in Alice Munro's 'Boys and Girls,'" *E-rea* (*Revue électronique d'études sur le monde Anglophone*) 12.1 | 2014, published online 15 December 2014, doi:10.4000/erea.4031

I am indebted to Michael Pflug for his generous permission to use Christiane Pflug's *Kitchen Door at Night II* to illustrate the cover of this book.

I would like to thank my friends and colleagues from the University of Franche-Comté for their support, in particular those in the English department and the CRIT EA 3224 research group (*Centre de recherches interdisciplinaires et transculturelles*); I have benefited greatly from their patience and encouragement over the years.

My affectionate thanks go to my family whose unconditional support has sustained me in my efforts.

And my deepest gratitude is to Lee Garner whose love, support, advice, and encouragement are written into every page of this work.

Preface

A work of extensive scholarship … is a labour of love. It is conceived in a spirit of passionate admiration and interest, propelled by a profound intellectual and emotional engagement … "Love" is not too strong a word to describe the impulse that inspires a scholar to devote many years of research to the work … of an author.

JoAnn McCaig, *Reading In*, xvi

Love, in the sense that McCaig gives it, is a form of identification with the "soul" of the text, or in other words, with its particular way of confronting the abyss at the heart of being. This book was born of two such loves, first for the stories of Alice Munro, and second for the psychoanalytic theory of Jacques Lacan. My conviction, in bringing them into dialogue, is that they approach the enigmas of human existence in different but mutually illuminating ways.

Alice Munro's stories entered my world in the late 1970s when I discovered her early collections; with the publication of each subsequent volume, I experienced anew the shock and pleasure of recognition that accompanies the reading of Munro. Her writing teases out the intricate, half-acknowledged complexities and emotional contradictions of human existence in such a way that they are unapologetically laid bare, to be acknowledged in their truth value, and as likely to be tinged with shame as jubilation.

Jacques Lacan's work belongs to another sphere entirely. I was introduced to his work by way of the well-known articles from his collected *Ecrits*; this was in the 1990s when I was working on a master's dissertation on Margaret Atwood's *Surfacing*. Lacan's writing and teaching revisits Freud's work in the light of twentieth-century theoretical developments. My interest in Lacan then remained dormant for some time, until around 2005 when I discovered the wealth of contemporary criticism being done on the basis of his theoretical insights. In my own terms, I became a Lacanian and, in the process, found a way to revisit the stories of Alice Munro, whose enigmatic configurations create a space of identification but so often seem to resist analytic criticism.

Munro's stories trace the contours of the opaque place *beyond* the pleasure principle, the place where *jouissance* infuses the text. Lacan's theory helps us recognize that place when we encounter it.

READING ALICE MUNRO WITH JACQUES LACAN

INTRODUCTION

The Black Room and the Opaque Place of Jouissance

The work of the writer and that of the psychoanalyst meet up at that point where each questions the fabric of meaning into which the fate of the human subject is woven, and where each locates the knots of the impossible-to-say in the experience of the speaking being. Literature and psychoanalysis, their discourses and written texts, meet up on the rim of the hole of the real that they delimit differently.

Ginette Michaux, *De Sophocle á Proust,* 25

The reader of a story by Alice Munro is drawn into the weave of conflicting hopes, desires, fantasies, shames, regrets, and absolutions that make up the lives of girls and women; of men too, but Munro's subject is, more than anything else, the inner lives of women and the ways in which they question their place in relation to others. Parents, lovers, and the uncanny other within are the recurrent, insistent partners in the Munrovian dialogues with the womanly self. Undertaken from a Lacanian perspective, this study of selected stories by Alice Munro sets out to explore these fields of feminine subjectivity, love, desire, and *jouissance*.

But first, why Lacan? What is the particular value of a Lacanian perspective? To begin with, it recognizes the central place of subjectivity in writing and defines subjectivity in a radically new way. The most widely accepted definitions of the human being conceive of men and women as entities divided between their creaturely animal nature and their thinking selves. This division leads on to others that always depend upon binary oppositions: male / female, animal / human, mind / body, with a certain degree of slippage accorded.[1] Questioning the degree of play between the antagonistic terms has been the motor force of recent or emerging critical schools (poststructuralism, gender studies, ecocriticism, posthumanism). However, these divisions are seen to be grounded outside the individual subject's being and are contingent on a point of comparison: the mind / body split depends upon a culture / biology division of knowledge; the male / female divide is a way of translating biological differences; the masculine / feminine is a way of accounting for social imprinting and cultural presuppositions. These categories render certain aspects of human existence intelligible but do not take into account the force, both destabilizing and creative, of the unconscious. In the Lacanian approach to human subjectivity, the human being is *differently* split; that is, the split is constitutive – the very effect of the intervention of language as formative of the emergent subject. Language "cuts" into the subject, transforming his / her libidinal, bodily jouissance, thereby binding it to the word. Rather than a being divided between language and the body, the Lacanian subject is a "speakingbeing" (*parlêtre* in French), a neologism that refuses hyphenation: bodily being and speaking subject are inextricably bound together, and what binds them is jouissance.

A multifaceted concept, jouissance is, first, an event of the body having to do with primal pleasure and pain, with the intensities of bodily affects.[2] Yet animal jouissance – the pure, unmediated jouissance of the body – is lost to us once we enter the realm of language. Henceforth our jouissance will be regulated by cultural laws, by the signifying cut, the marking of language, and the fixation of libidinal orientations that will affect the ongoing course of our subjective destiny. This is not a minor part of our being, but rather the closest thing we have to an "essence": not a given, but an indelible tracing of libidinal furrows, the laying down of "letters"[3] that define us and anchor those signifiers that, for each of us, matter most: those that command our intimate sense of who we are.

However, the cut of language is not a clean severing; it leaves a remainder that Lacan calls *objet a*. This mythical object is what is left over from the intervention of the word; if language cuts us from animal plenitude (which might also be expressed as the ignorance of our mortality), it leaves intact, or perhaps produces, the dream of a supposed lost fullness of pleasure of being. A retroactive dream of recovering something that never really existed, the objet a is a desire-causing lack stitched into the subjective fabric of our selves, to haunt us and taunt us from within.

This haunting objet a, which does not "exist," nevertheless *ex-sists*, or "insists … from the outside" (Lacan, *SXX* 22, translator's note 24) in the sense that, as that which names our constitutive lack, it has subjective effects: it creates the space of a wanting, or in other words, of desire itself. In this perspective, the objet a is, according to Lacan, the object-*cause* of desire. As the lack we carry within us, it is not an object *separate* from, but *separable* from the subject in that it propels desire forward and can be construed as a mediator between the subject and others. Never recognizing that the split *is* its being, the subject follows the metonymic path of desire, projecting its objet a onto a series of substitute objects of satisfaction but never arriving at the end of desire, which has no "final" object since desire is, in its structure and dynamics, always a *desire for something else*.

In the shape of its substitute forms, the objet a lends the human subject the support of fantasy, the fantasy that "some thing" might make it whole. In seeking out a partner, the subject embarks on the adventures of desire, jouissance, and love but never achieves wholeness, for the subject is, irremediably, split. It is the split – the lack, the constitutive signifying cut from mythical plenitude, the fall into language – that defines subjectivity; without the recognition of this constitutive *lack-in-being*, no truth of subjectivity can be approached. This is the Lacanian orientation on human subjectivity.

The stories of Alice Munro structure this lack-in-being into the narrative destinies of their characters. Images of that lack abound as her stories embrace the whole of human experience in its different stages; from childhood to late adulthood, Munro's characters confront the enigmas of desire, of love, and of the lacking self. They are unsettled by the libidinal resonance of language, by their often unwanted fantasies, and, especially, by what might be seen as the "beyond" of fantasy, where jouissance, glimpsed *as if* untouched by language, as if one literally could encounter the mythical lost object, reveals its morbid dimension.

The three stories analyzed in the first section of this volume focus on the early formative years of the subject; they are stories of childhood. The analyses of "Royal Beatings" and "Princess Ida" deal with the ways in which, even at the presignifying level that Lacan calls *lalangue*, language resonates and furrows pathways of jouissance in the child's subjective "becoming." Moreover, the parental couple, whose mythical status is ironically inscribed in the titles of these two stories, is given its due as the first significant representatives of the Other the child encounters. The parents constitute the primary locus of the child's encounter with desire: first, with their desire for her *to be*, and second, with their desire for her to be *something*. In each of these stories, the child is shaped by this necessarily enigmatic parental desire, but she also resists it, forging and finding the coordinates of her own constitutive desire.

While the scope of Lacanian investigation comprises the entire field of human subjectivity, in the context of the present study, a preliminary remark on the question of feminine subjectivity might be useful. The overarching Lacanian premise is that subjectivity is constituted by the Borromean knotting of the psychic orders of the symbolic, the imaginary, and the real, which organize the subject's insertion in language. To state the matter very broadly at this point, language comes to us from the *symbolic* order, which is the register of signifiers, codes, and laws; the *imaginary* is the field of images, the place of projection of a self-image, and the mode of seeing oneself being seen by the Other; the *real* is what resists integration into these orders – it is the manifestation of the limits, impossibilities, and failures of language, but also, notably, of jouissance. But the question of subjectivity can only really be posed as *sexed* subjectivity; in other words, the signifier "subject" refers to an individual who has confronted the law of culture, the fundamental NO that frustrates the aspiration to be or have it all (to be "all" for the mother, to have the mother "all" to oneself, to be allowed unhampered jouissance without regard for the Other), and this confrontation with the law of culture is called symbolic castration. Included in the "all" that this psychic moment forbids is the "all" of sexual identity: within human culture, no subjective position is liveable (in the sense of bearable) without resolving, in some way or another, the question "Am I a boy or a girl?" As I will argue in my analysis of Munro's "Boys and Girls," which closes the first section, the grounding moment that gives access to adult subjectivity takes the form of an "act" – an unconscious choice, in this case, to assume a mode of being, or in other words, a sexed position, in relation to the law. Not unrelated to this question of the law of symbolic castration is Lacan's refusal of the universal Woman in favour of a conceptualization of woman as "not-whole," or "not-all"; that is, women are not wholly defined by the phallic signifier, the signifier of the law of the symbolic order. This requires a word more of explanation.

If the being of "man" is based on the phallic exception that establishes the universal law (following Freud's myth of the father of the primal horde [*Totem and Taboo*]), the being of a woman is different. Neither wholly captured by the universal, nor yet outside of it, a woman is situated in a particular way through oedipal castration in her relation to the Other: she is situated as *not-all* within the sphere of the signifier. In other words, she is not wholly encompassed by the limit of the phallically grounded universal law of the symbolic order, and retains the *possibility* of an Other jouissance, an experience of a sort of limitlessness correlated to the unconscious knowledge that the universal "man" is lacking, that the grounding premises of the symbolic order have the structure of a fiction, or of a functional (and as Freud's allegory exemplifies, a libidinally motivated) myth. At the level of language, this inconsistency in the symbolic order goes by the formula S(Ⱥ), to be read "the signifier of the lack in the Other." This place where the Other of the signifier is lacking, where it is revealed as having no final referent – since there *is* no Other of the Other – is the "opaque place of *jouissance*" (Lacan, *SXX* 82); it is there where the symbolic meets the real, or one might say, encounters its undoing. It is a singular place, empty of meaning, where words, in the jouissance that saturates them, speak not of their shared symbolic meaning but of "the specific value the subject gives to [them]" (Soler, *Lacan* ch. 17): this space is marked out differently in each of us, through the letter of the lalangue. It is the place of the falling away of meaning, but also of new creations, sublimations, and love.

These theoretical remarks will raise more questions than provide answers for those who are unfamiliar with Lacanian theory, and I have therefore taken care to mark the theoretical trail in more detail in each of the analyses, so as to clarify the issues under discussion.[4] This is the case in the first group of readings, but perhaps even more so in the analyses of stories in the second half of this volume – "Eskimo" and "Too Much Happiness," which deal more frontally with Munro's exploration of feminine fantasy, desire, and jouissance, and "Tell Me Yes or No," which explores the complexities and enigmas of love. The epilogue to these analyses, entitled "The Truth of the Fixion," looks over the analytic ground covered and questions whether certain symptomatic traits of writing can be discerned through their persistence and insistence in the works of Munro.

But fundamentally, how can one *read* psychoanalytically? There will be no question of psychobiography here. Nor is it sufficient to decipher or "interpret" the text; although this is a necessary first step, an interpretation is in itself a language construction, a new text that may in turn be interpreted, and so forth, in a metonymic process of thickening rather than clarifying the text (Miller, "Reading a Symptom"). My intention here is not to inflate the stories by adding another fiction to them, but rather to approach their irreducible point of resistance to meaning, which is marked by a void. Halpern notes that "for Lacan, *all* art incorporates a void which signifies its approach to the Thing," and quotes from Lacan's *SVII*: "This Thing, all forms of which created by man belong to the sphere of sublimation, this Thing will always be represented by emptiness, precisely because it cannot be represented by anything else – or more exactly, because it can only be represented by something else. But in every form of sublimation, emptiness is determinative … All art is characterized by a certain mode of organization around this emptiness" (160). The site of this emptiness also goes by the name of the opaque place of jouissance; from there springs both creation and destruction. Approaching its inscription in the text can be achieved only by following the text to where it articulates its truth symptomatically: "The discipline of reading targets the materiality of writing, i.e. the letter in so far as it produces the event of jouissance that is decisive for the formation of symptoms. Knowing how to read targets this initial shock" (Miller, "Reading a Symptom").

The hope of final resolution, however, needs to be abandoned from the start: for Lacan, the symptom, because of the jouissance that sustains it, preserves a degree of opacity in that it excludes meaning ("Joyce le symptôme" 570). About the truth, a written text cannot, any more than speech can, say everything: "I always speak the truth. Not the whole truth, because there's no way, to say it all. Saying it all is literally impossible: words fail. Yet it's through this very impossibility that the truth holds onto the real" (*Television* 3). Where the truth is concerned, all one can do is "run after it," says Lacan in his preface to the English edition of *Seminar XI* (vii). To do so, we need to be attentive to the structural function of the "letter that never betrays its content but gives shape to the libidinal logic by which the subject is determined." The "letter" in this sense is related to the primary signifier, a signifier (or signifier-cluster) without signification, the one in the text that marks the place of the lack-in-being of subjectivity, the place of the real of the drive, around which the text takes form: "The idea of 'sublimated *jouissance*' forces us to look closer at what Lacan has to say about the 'letter,' and letters in general, as providing a rim, a margin encircling the erotic hole left by *jouissance*" (Rabaté, *Jacques Lacan* 28). Where sublimation, the letter, and a symptomatic reading are concerned, the text may be likened to "[the] formal envelope of the symptom, that is, … what gives Symbolic form to the Real of the drive. Thus considered, the symptom is a Symbolic construction built around a Real kernel of jouissance. In Freud's words, it is 'like the grain of sand around which an oyster forms its pearl'" (Verhaeghe and Declercq 3). Writers use different metaphors to indicate this kernel of jouissance, this point of impossibility, "whose unbearable, terrible Good is also an Evil" (Halpern).[5]

The analyses undertaken here point to some of Munro's narrative pearls of jouissance. That *something* in a story must mark the place of this enigmatic spot of good and evil is made explicit by Munro in her essay "What Is Real?" when she comments that the beating of Mr Tyde in "Royal Beatings" constitutes the "black room at the centre of the house," the room that encompasses the "indescribable feeling that is like the soul of the story" (226, 224). Each story has, in some form, its own "black room." To get there, and to make the way there intelligible, is the whole project of this book.

Throughout the chapters to follow, I engage as honestly as possible with the workings of the texts and their symptomatic singularity, where the signature of their "saying" is encoded in the repetitions, blockages, intensities, contradictions, and signifiers of desire that circle round, sketch out, and point toward the place of obscure jouissance. It is in the light of this logic of analysis that I focus on individual stories, on a particular knot of subjectivity or a symptom; in my view, that is where Munro's genius lies – in her ability to go unflinchingly and with "outstanding lucidity" (Albertazzi 42) to the core of a particular symptomatic moment of subjectivity. For this reason, her work resists synthesis: her stories do not *produce* meaning, they pare it down to the bare bones and allow for the emergence of intimate truths, none of which is ever "it," the final answer or concluding statement.

Ultimately, the reader would be disappointed to achieve such a resolution: it is because the jouissance that sustains the symbolic and imaginary registers is veiled in fantasy that the stories are compelling. Indeed, jouissance needs to be cloaked in fantasy even to be approachable;[6] fantasy opens up the space of desire, and it is the movement of desire itself that is satisfying. Munro's writing structurally reflects this; her stories constantly bring into confrontation the mismatching of discordant desires, thereby keeping them alive rather than satiated; her narratives are shaped by the exploration of the obstacles to satisfaction. The encounter with these obstacles paradoxically produces, on occasion, a contradictory sort of happiness.

From the earliest period of her writing, Munro's stories have borne witness to the unspeakable pleasure of approaching the point of human obscurity where all meaning might be extinguished. I will conclude these introductory remarks with an analysis of a passage from "Images" belonging to Munro's first collection, *Dance of the Happy Shades*; it takes the reader to one such encounter as well as pointing toward several of the thematic and theoretical directions that will be marked out and followed in the coming chapters.

In "Images," a young girl accompanies her father as he goes out to check his muskrat traps. As they advance along the path, an effect of uncanny strangeness is produced when the girl focuses on her father's boots, seeing them as a metonymic extension of her father's whole person: "My father's boots went ahead ... They had an expression that was dogged and uncompromising, even brutal, and I thought of that as part of my father's look, the counterpart of his readiness for jokes and courtesies. Nor did that brutality surprise me; my father came back to us always" (36). The potentially brutal otherness of the father is both recognized and, immediately afterwards, neutralized. Recognition and denial are similarly at work when one of the traps is discovered with a muskrat in it and the father is seen "mercifully drowning" it. Such contradictions as these – the laying side by side of the "brutal" and the "courteous" in the father, and the giving of death as an act of kindness – arouse, or at least accompany, a surge of both fear and longing in the child: "I only wanted, but did not dare, to touch the stiff, soaked body, a fact of death" (36).

The fact of death, thus far, remains distanced from the girl's subjective self by its projection onto the animal; the power over life and death that the father literally wields is similarly contemplated at one remove, shielded by his more civilized, courteous social self and by the practical aspects of trapping animals, as well as by his daughter's trust in him. The story then opens up a space that confronts the child with the power of the Other, and with the unconscionable *temptation* of the subject to assent to it completely. In keeping with her lack of surprise at her father's potential for "brutality," the girl is "not surprised" at the completely unexpected image that appears before her – that of a man in the woods, with an axe:

> The man crossed my path somewhere ahead, continuing down to the river. People say they have been paralyzed by fear, but I was transfixed, as if struck by lightning, and what hit me did not feel like fear so much as recognition. I was not surprised. This is the sight that does not surprise you, the thing you have always known was there that comes so naturally, moving delicately and contentedly and in no hurry, as if it was made, in the first place, from a wish of yours, a hope of something final, terrifying … And I never thought, or even hoped for, anything but the worst. (37)

The bodily impact of being "transfixed," supported by the image of being "struck" or "hit" by something both unforeseen and yet, already known, marks the place of jouissance in the story. Fatal, yet ambiguously "hoped for," taking form through "a wish," even for the worst (death, the possibility of one's own annihilation), this image is the place of "recognition" for the child in this narrative. Elements of the scene have been foreshadowed in the text, so that recognition also strikes the reader: the "gleaming" aspect of the "little axe, or hatchet" (37) held by the man points back to the luminosity of the "slim bright blade" of her father's skinning knife glimpsed by the child earlier in the story. In this way, the menacing stranger is transformed into a form of familiar, a shadow-version of her father.[7]

At work here, as in other stories, is the interplay between the main character and the significant others who enter her fantasy world and become, in their imaginary, symbolic, and real incarnations, part of her *extimate* reality. They embody something "so exterior (yet so intimate) to the logic of the subject that it is not even repressed; it is rather 'a primordial function which is located at the level of the initial establishment of ... Unconscious [representations]'" (Halpern).[8] In this extimate place of subjectivity, the outside world of "reality" reveals itself to the young girl in the story as, following Lacan, "strange and even hostile on occasion," spewing up, as in this passage, "an object" (here, a man with an axe) that "corresponds to the one the subject represents to [her]self at that moment" (Lacan, *SVII* 62) and presenting it as there, as always having been there, already known on some level, waiting to be recognized. Beyond their function at the realist level of the story, the gleaming knife of the father and the bright blade of the axe have been metaphorically spewed up from the place of jouissance, which is marked in the story by a spot on the river, "silver in the middle where the sun hit it and where it arrowed in to its swiftest motion"; the sunlit current becomes the indicator of "some hidden place where the water issued with a roar from underground," a sound "not loud but deep" (36–7). From this place, both illuminated and hidden, emerges an image of something to be situated "in relation to the world of wishes and expectations" (Lacan, *SVII* 62), a stain of the jouissance of the real cloaked in the fantasy of a murderous man who functions as a sign pointing toward the primordial lost object, the simultaneously good and evil objet a that marks our mortal existence and that can never be "found again" because it is no object in particular. And yet, "some *thing* is there while one waits for something better, or something worse: something that one wants" (Lacan, *SVII* 63).[9] This is what Munro's writing knows.

1

Early Encounters with the Other

"Royal Beatings"

Fantasy, Desire, and Pickled Arseholes

The enigmas that define the questioning impulse at work in childhood are central to Alice Munro's "Royal Beatings." More specifically, the story weaves its double-stranded narrative around the enigma of origins: the origins of the parental desire that presided over the child's coming into being, and the place opened up in the world for the child through that desire. The permanence of that desire is challenged in the course of the narrative, and the possibility of its negation is formulated, so that it might be confronted.

The story takes shape around the position of a preadolescent girl named Rose, whose point of view focuses the narrative. She is situated within a family of the 1940s in which the dead mother's place has been taken up by the stepmother, named Flo. The father's presence is mainly on the margins, as he carries out his furniture repair work in a shed behind the house, out of reach of the daily squabbles between Flo and Rose; his emergence from the shed, on Flo's request, to administer a beating to Rose, is the story's central, pulsating event. This is indeed the point by which many critics try to grasp this story, which is rich in narrative complexity, energetic undercurrents, and sparks of linguistic inventiveness. Yet, taken in isolation, this episode becomes overdetermined, and is often reduced to a further index of patriarchal social violence. Howells, for example, comments: "It is a case where private domestic violence parodies and lays bare the brutality of physical punishment" (53). This may be true, but it is certainly not what makes the beating scene fascinating.

Carrington, one of the most analytic readers of Munro, gets closer to the core of the story in pointing out that the beating, while inscribed within the realistic level of the narrative, has the structure of a fantasy. Referring to Munro's qualification of "Royal Beatings" as "the story about the child being beaten," Carrington turns to Freud's essay on beating fantasies, "A Child Is Being Beaten," and then follows Freud's argument through its different stages, offering a convincing analysis of the erotic variability in some of Munro's stories from "pleasure in watching a beating" to "pleasure in being beaten," the latter being experienced as both "punishment for the forbidden genital relation" and as "regressive substitute for it" (Carrington 42–8).

Acknowledging this reading as a useful starting point, I would like to investigate this fantasy world of "Royal Beatings" more closely by expanding the question outwards to the unconscious structuring of the story; that is to say, the ways in which not just the beating, but the story as a whole allow us to approach the emergence of the desiring subject. On this royal road, aspects of the mythical family romance, the language of the unconscious, multiple versions of the father, and the question of the beating fantasy will be encountered.

THE ROYAL FAMILY

The myths and tales of childhood give shape to the anxiety that growing up involves, and indeed, the fairy tale component is clearly present from the very start of the story when Rose gives an account of her origins. This aspect of the narrative follows the classical form of childhood family romance fantasies: "[They] center on the idea that one's parents are not really one's parents, but that one is the child of some exalted personage, and that, due to unfortunate circumstances, one has been reduced to living with these people, who *claim* to be one's parents … often only one parent is thought to be a false one … a step-parent" (Bettelheim 68). Rose's story, as unconscious fantasy, might therefore be read as follows: My parents appear as powerful figures in my world. My father is the King – "king of the royal beatings" (3) – and Flo is the (necessarily wicked) stepmother who took the place of my loving and kind "true" mother who died and who now belongs to my memories of "an orderly, far gentler … time" (4).

I am generally kept away from my father, "who had a shed out behind the store, where he worked at his furniture repairing and restoring" (4), and am therefore at the service of my wicked stepmother who doesn't love me, but loves her true child, my half-brother, Brian.

Flo appears in this scenario as a narrative device allowing Rose to express hostility toward the feminine rival in her oedipal desire for recognition from the father. By aiming her antipathy at this "false mother," Rose distracts us from the fairy-tale embodiment of the stepmother as the expulsed, unwanted part of the mother: "The fantasy of the wicked stepmother not only preserves the good mother intact, it also prevents having to feel guilty about one's angry thoughts and wishes about her … [Furthermore, it] helps the child not to be devastated by experiencing the mother as evil" (Bettelheim 69). If Flo is unambiguously defined as a stepmother in the story, there are nonetheless traces of the "other" mother in her, in the form of a duality (and durability) of impression: "Rose's earliest memories of Flo were of extraordinary softness and hardness" (11).

Within this framework, it is perfectly coherent that Rose's relationship to Flo should be described as a "struggle" (15), a "wrangle" that "has been going on forever, like a dream that goes back and back into other dreams, over hills and through doorways, maddeningly dim and populous and familiar and elusive" (13). There is a constant slipping away, of time and space, of people and purpose in the phrasing of this proposition that points us toward the unconscious where "thoughts"[1] are "elusive," "dim" and yet "familiar" to the subject, appearing in dreams in disguised form. The dream referred to here is an anxious one, where the object of the wrangle can never be found, caught, or even located. The indeterminate cause of the anxiety allows it to expand and cover everything that Flo touches, so that a gap opens up between what is and what appears to be. In other words, within Rose's fantasy structure, Flo is an imposter, the usurper of her mother's place; she came "to take over Rose" (4) and remove her from her rightful house by transforming it into a store: "the store was really a house" (3). And if a house can become a store, and a good mother can become a "bad" mother, then perhaps she herself is not what she believes. Is she really the child of her parents? After all, she did not inherit their traits: "From both parents Rose should have inherited clever hands, a quick sympathy with materials, an eye for the nicest turns of mending, but she hadn't" (3). Did she perhaps end up in the wrong family? Is she, too, an imposter, an ugly duckling who hatched from the "hard-boiled egg in [her] mother's chest" to be found, like Moses, "a baby in a basket" (4), separated from her true destiny? And if she is not legitimate, then do her parents really love her? No child escapes these existential questions. "Royal Beatings" does not answer them, but rather sublimates them, transforms them into the fantasy that shapes and structures them.

LANGUAGE AND LALANGUE

The possibility that people, even those most familiar to us, might be imposters living double lives is supported by a doubleness that characterizes Rose's developing perception of the world. Seeing the world around her as divided between private and public spheres, she makes no connection between the person in the flimsy-walled kitchen-corner bathroom "creating the noises" and the "person who walked out" (6), nor between the respectable town of Hanratty, with its doctors, lawyers, and lay workers, and the poorer area of West Hanratty with its "large improvident families of casual bootleggers and prostitutes and unsuccessful thieves" (6). An acknowledged level of reality, seen as respectable, is thereby held in place by denying or marginalizing its shadow version, seen as abject. The people associated with the acknowledged realm of the public sphere would be subject to expectations of propriety and would therefore potentially be open to accusations of "foolishness, and showiness, and self-approbation" (12); the private sphere, on the other hand, is unmentionable (as attested by phrases such as "She could never ask him," or "no reference was made" [6]), but it produces effects that Rose experiences as both "dangerous" and "delightful" (14).

The doubleness of experience "out there" is also operative within the speaking subject at the level of the opposition between language as communicable and lalangue as presignifying. To say that the subject is a speaking being means that he or she has been formed by language, which, in itself, may be situated in relation to the three psychic registers: the symbolic (the social bond), the imaginary (the subject's fantasized point of insertion into the social world), and the real (that which escapes the possibilities of symbolization in language – that for which we have no words – but which nonetheless affects the subject). These different psychic orders – the symbolic, the imaginary, and the real – find their expression in utterance in different ways: the symbolic speaks the language of intelligible communication and exchange, underpinned by communally recognized values and laws. The imaginary is "symptomatic" language, carrying the stamp of the subject's self-image; it is the site of dyadic love and hate, similarity and rivalry. The real is the place where that symptomatic, imaginary self is rooted: in the earliest impressions and ambiguities emerging from the relation to one's "mother" tongue: the music, eruptions, sound impressions, and all the raw material of language, but also their associations with the pleasures and pains experienced in the process of their imprinting in the psyche; this is what Lacan calls lalangue.[2] Language is intelligible, shared, and communal; lalangue is unique to each subject, a sort of *fingerprint* of unorganized language elements stamped on the psyche in the process of subjectification. The subject, singular in her insertion into a nonetheless communal language, having encountered lalangue in a unique time, place, and individual context, has one foot in each. Where language gives us signifiers with intelligible (and yet equivocal) signifieds, lalangue gives us the "letter," which for Lacan is in the real, since it is not meaningful in spite of its subjective effects; it is "associated not with unconscious meaning or signifying effects discernible in the symbolic but with affects or 'being-effects' of the (m)Other tongue" (Barnard, *Tongues* 183). According to Fink, lalangue, as "garbled speech and conflated words, bring[s] us closer to the 'stuff' of language than well articulated phrases, and serve[s] as something of a bridge between the symbolic and the real" (*The Lacanian Subject* 29). In this sense, lalangue is perhaps the persistent trace of the early stages of symbolization, when the relative fixity of later symbolic meaning has not yet weighted down the words for the child.

These questions of the tension between language and its unconscious effects are central to "Royal Beatings" and can be considered in relation to at least three of the narrative's events, beginning with the title itself. "Royal Beatings" comes to function as a unified signifier: "royalbeatings," a sound-impression that thickens out in Rose's mind and presents itself not as meaningful, but as a challenge to meaning. In its effects, it cannot be assimilated: royal and beating cannot ever come together satisfactorily to account for Flo's use of it; when she habitually announces "You are going to get one Royal Beating," to Rose "the word Royal lolled on Flo's tongue" (3), which is, to all intents and purposes, the "mother('s) tongue" in the story. The sound-phrase is in excess of any literal meaning one might construe. Rose strives to give consistency to this signifier whose meaning is unsettled in her mind: its dominant effect is the paradoxical conflation of high and low where "royalbeating" becomes a primal oxymoronic challenge to Rose's attempts to follow the path of reason: "how is a beating royal?" (3). This antithetical questioning colours the whole of her commentary on it: "She came up with a tree-lined avenue, a crowd of formal spectators, some white horses and black slaves. Someone knelt, and the blood came leaping out like banners. An occasion both savage and splendid. In real life they didn't approach such dignity, and it was only Flo who tried to supply the event with some high air of necessity and regret" (3). Thus, the oppositions white / black, savage / splendid, and necessity / regret preserve "royalbeating" in its paradoxical status.

The impossibility of making intelligible meaning out of words heard and even addressed to her attune Rose to the pleasure of circling round the impossible, which is to say the real. What is most real in the Lacanian sense, about the speakingbeing, is the drive: "If we ask 'Where does the drive come from?' we have only one answer: the drive is produced by the operation … of language … The *drive derives* from needs, the drive is a transformation produced by language of natural necessities, through the obligation of articulating demands. Such is the Lacanian thesis without which no one can be called a Lacanian: language is not an instrument that we can use as we want [but] is fundamentally inscribed in the real" (Soler, "Paradoxes" 90–1), in the enjoyment of the presignifying letter. In its relationship to the drives, language makes "something like a hole in the real, something that creates a will to jouissance, a constant pressing toward satisfaction" (Soler, "Paradoxes" 91). This mixture of paradoxical language-lalangue-drives-satisfaction is evident in Rose's chanting of her favourite rhyming couplet: "Two Vancouvers fried in snot! / Two pickled arseholes tied in a knot!" (14).

The lines proclaim themselves emphatically ("!") as meaningless. Steeped in the pleasure of verbal sound-play, nonmeaning is not in this case the unfulfilled anticipation of meaning, but a satisfying refusal of meaning itself. Whereas language, the language of the social bond, of the symbolic order, attempts to make up for the absence of any grounding for meaning in the universe – for the fact that there is no Other of the Other – by filling in the gap in the Other as best it can with words, words, words, offering the illusion of the existence of a final Word, this bit of nonsense, Rose's ditty, pokes its finger through the "hole" to make it visible. That it follows syntax, meter, and rhyme does not stop it from being nonsense since the words won't cooperate: it is the contrast between the syntactical promise of meaning (subject, verb, and object stand in their correct places) and the absurdity of the proposition itself that is exhilarating. Oddly enough, it is because it doesn't "mean" that it can be "read." It can be read, not for a message, but for effects, *jouissance* effects, the effects of the body caught up in language. How so?

To begin with, there are "two" Vancouvers. Asking Flo a question she knows the answer to – "what is a Vancouver?" (14), Rose takes pleasure in underlining the impossibility, the nonsense of "two Vancouvers." Vancouver as a proper name names the one Vancouver. And what is this impossibly doubled Vancouver doing? Being fried in snot. The breakdown of meaning is under way … Snot. Bodily excretions, prepared in a culinary mode: "pickled arseholes," the anal and the oral in one fell swoop. A city transformed into an eroticized body and, moreover, "Tied in a knot." Knot-not; Snot-'*s not*. Impossibilities are suggested, along with the intensities of their articulation: "speech concerns jouissance" (Lacan, *SXX* 112).

The pleasure Rose takes in circling round the oral and anal drives, cooking them up and tying them together is palpable, as is the multi-appendaged drive-creatures she substitutes for the Vancouvers further on, seeing them "shaped rather like octopuses, twitching in the pan" so as to prolong and vary her pleasure in the celebration of the polymorphous drives. The insistence of the drives in the unconscious is witnessed by Rose's comment that she "couldn't stop herself" (12) from chanting the lines, and yet the pleasure of the drives is not direct; it is channelled into speech.

Both Flo's "one Royal Beating" (3) and Rose's "Two Vancouvers" (14) offer challenges to reason, and therefore to language's claim to render the world meaningful. They are also inscribed in the child's dialectic of negotiation with parental desire: language has effects, and one of them is to provoke parental disapproval. In the case of the "Vancouvers," Rose's deliberate chanting just below the threshold of Flo's hearing is a form of provocation, the sort that leads precisely to the threat of the royal beating. This threat is Flo's response to the open display of the drives in their nonsensical vitality. Yet, the very process of trying to make meaning out of the available signifiers corresponds to the child's need to resolve the question *What do my parents want of me?* For a child, the first experience of the signifier is one of alienation since she enters this already-constituted language dimension out of nowhere. To begin with,

> the subject *exists* – insofar as the word has wrought him or her from nothingness, and he or she can be spoken of, talked about, and discoursed upon – yet remains beingless. Prior to the onset of alienation there was not the slightest question of being: "it's the subject himself who is not there to begin with" (quote from Lacan, *SIV*, 16 November 1966); afterwards his or her being is strictly potential. *Alienation gives rise to a pure possibility of being,* a place where one might expect to find a subject, but which nevertheless remains empty. Alienation engenders, in a sense, a place in which it is clear that there is, as of yet, no subject: a place where something is conspicuously lacking. *The subject's first guise is this very lack.* (Fink, *The Lacanian Subject* 51–2)

This place of lack is the one marked out for the child by the parental desire that brought him or her into existence. Beyond this presubjective state of potential being, subjectivity is conceivable in the second phase, that of "separation," which "consists in the attempt by the alienated subject to come to grips with [the] Other's desire as it manifests itself in the subject's world" (Fink, *The Lacanian Subject* 50). We might therefore understand Rose's word games and acute awareness of language effects as an index of that movement from alienation toward separation, toward the assumption of her subjectivity. Subverting meaning through word play, trying to conjure up a meaning for that "royalbeating" that stands in for the idea of parental power, is an attempt to avoid being pinned down by its effects.

Caught up in the daily "household struggle" (15) with Flo, Rose is inundated by the "flo(w)" of her words; she is affected by them and tries to give them meaning. She hears Flo singing, "Oh the buzzin' of the bees in the cigarette trees / And the soda-*water* fountain" (12). There is no readily available unity of meaning to this folk song; it is evocative rather than explicative. It has the formal features of a lilting rhythm, dense alliteration, emphasis, and so forth, but where Rose is concerned, its meaning is in its effect, the first of which is to make Flo more loveable: "oral transmission engenders love and … love and knowledge are not unrelated" (Fink, *Lacan to the Letter* 68). Through her songs, Flo offers herself as an object to be loved, and what she can be loved for is what she would not, in her fully conscious selfhood, acknowledge: her secret knowledge of nature and sexuality, joy, hardiness, and even a delight in the impossible (cigarette trees): "Rose heard in her voice the reckless dangerous life of cities, the gum-chewing sharp answers" (12). It is in these never-admitted to, but unwittingly revealed possibilities that Rose can situate her affection toward Flo.

Similarly, the second song that Rose "remembers" from Flo affects her: "Then slowly, slowly, she got up / And slowly she came nigh him / And all she said, that she ever did say / Was young man, I think you're dying" (12). Here are intimations of death and sexuality intertwined, and "all kinds of outrages and sorrows jumbled up together in it" (12). Flo's voice insinuates itself into Rose's developing subjectivity through a series of melodious, enigmatic, paradoxical allusions to a world of confused desires, losses, and possibilities. Speech speaks the lalangue of the drives, gives utterance to the jouissance with which language binds itself to the subject, in a dialectics of lack and desire. Flo sings openly, her words are unfettered, there for the taking; Rose chants in the mode of transgression, for pleasure and for provocation, the two women voicing an undercurrent of affective being. But what of the father's voice? To answer the question we need first to ask another: which father?

THE KING'S SPEECH

"Royal Beatings" belongs to the collection originally entitled *Who Do You Think You Are?*[3] and indeed, the question of identity is posed for each character, but nowhere do we see a greater fragmentation of identity than in the figure of the father. To begin with, there are two "fathers" in the story: Rose's, and in the story-within-the-story, Becky Tyde's father, rumoured to be a child beater. But even if we limit ourselves for the moment to the individual case of Rose's father, there are several facets to him, each of which affects Rose in a particular way. There is the wordplay father whose fondness for the sonority of language affiliates him with the sphere of the mother; there is the symbolic father, the King, a placeholder for the neutrality of the law; and there is the imaginary father, the actual man who attempts to fill this symbolic space and who, in his subjective incarnation, can never really achieve the neutrality the function requires, falling either into excessive adherence to, or into total abandonment of the law he represents. All of these figures are fathers-for-Rose, they are versions of the father (or to play with Lacan's pun, père-versions) that she confronts in her fairy tale account of the origins of her "self."

The Father as (m)Other

Rose encounters the father's lalangue-babble, heard rather than seen, coming "from the shed" (5). In Lacan's revision of Freud's theory of the drives, the voice is a partial drive-object and is related to desire: the father's voice, the voice of parental desire, is a riddle for the child – *What do they want of me? What do they want me to be? Do they want me at all?* – that makes itself heard or felt in the ear. From behind the closed door emerges "not only coughing, but speech, a continual muttering, reproachful or encouraging, usually just below the level at which separate words could be made out … Now and then some words would break through and hang clear and nonsensical on the air … 'Macaroni, pepperoni, Botticelli, beans –'" (5).[4] This disembodied voice of the father is indeed enigmatic; Rose immediately asks herself "What could that mean?" (6). It is not dismissed as meaningless; rather, it is interrogated as enigmatic and worth keeping: "Rose used to repeat such things to herself" (6), delighting perhaps in their Italian exoticism and in the suggestion of the oral drive that emerges here through the food lexicon, as in her own song of fried Vancouvers. Unmoored to any social meaning, such words can "hang" in the air, to be plucked by Rose, a treasure to tuck away in her storehouse of signifiers: this is the father's unwitting, even unwilling, gift: "When he realized they were out, there would be a quick bit of cover-up coughing, a swallowing, an alert, unusual silence" (5). The father *knows* that his role as symbolic father, that is, as the embodiment of the paternal metaphor, is to guard the "language" of social contract and of intelligible meaning, not the associative, "mother"-tongue wordplay of lalangue. Indeed, when Rose says that the "person who spoke these words and the person who spoke to her as her father, were not the same" (6), she is right – the murmuring poet of the work shed is not in the role of the father; rather, at that moment, he embodies the function of the mother tongue, offering his daughter, in the very air that circulates between them, sounds that imprint themselves on her: alliterations, associations, and rhythms that affect her, suggesting, moving toward, but never achieving or arriving at their potential to cohere and produce meaning.

The Mystical Father

It is in this sense that Rose intuitively understands that if she were caught in the act of seeing him not "seeming" to be the father, she "would not be forgiven" (6). It would, by the fact of itself, undermine his authority, since his embodiment of that authority depends upon his *appearing to embody it without self-division*. He must make (others) believe that he is wholly that.

Knowing that she must not reveal to the king that he is naked, Rose is nonetheless fascinated and stunned by what emerges from this gap in seeming-wholeness: "The cloud-capped towers, she heard him say once. / 'The cloud-capped towers, the gorgeous palaces'" (6). Exiled in his work shed, the father is likened to the banished Prospero, reciting words that evoke both the beauty – "gorgeous" – of the constitutive illusions of life and their ephemeral and dramatic – "cloud-capped" – nature; in this way, he stamps his intuition of the tragic beauty of impossible aspirations and inevitable loss on Rose: "That was like a hand clapped against [her] chest, not to hurt, but to astonish her, to take her breath away" (6). From the father's speech to the daughter's hearing, there is displacement and condensation in the shift from "cloud-capped" to "hand clapped," where the central letters of cl$_{\text{oud-c}}$apped fall away, striking Rose in the chest, as her body applauds the father's performance in the repetition of the line. The *shock of the real*, "the material encounter between a signifier and the body, the pure shock of language on the body" (Miller, "Reading a Symptom"), is where the unconscious emerges, briefly, fleetingly, pulsatingly, and then recedes. Now Rose flees: "She had to run then, she had to get away" (6), not to save her father from his fall – she *knows*, even if she hides her knowledge from him, that that is constitutive – but from herself, from the experience of the self-division of her own being that has knocked the wind out of her, from the "dissolve" to come in Prospero's speech.[5]

The literary intertext for the father's words situates him within the symbolic order, the order of transmissible language, but the words themselves evoke the point at which meaning fails: the moment when they become poetically charged precisely because they suggest the limits of comprehension and circle the fundamental mysteries of being – origin and end. The father, too, is a writer, and interrogates the mysteries of existence, even if, as is often the case with Munro, the comparison is bathetic. What does he write? After his death, some of the father's notes are discovered in his shed: accounts and receipts, but also observations, things "he had been moved to write down" (4):

> Ate new potatoes 25th June. Record.
> Dark Day, 1880's, nothing supernatural. Clouds of ash from forest fires.
> Aug 16, 1938. Giant thunderstorm in evng. Lightning str. Pres. Church,
> Turberry Twp. Will of god?
> Scald strawberries to remove acid.
> All things are alive. Spinoza. (5)

What the father signifies, in this desire to leave a trace of the things that "moved" him, is perhaps the desire for a *beyond* of human existence. In the mixture of the everyday and the extraordinary, the empirical and the superstitious, we discern a yearning for or a leaning toward something that infuses the banal with inscrutable meaning: "Record," "supernatural," "giant," "lightning," "god" all bear witness to an openness to the immanence of the unaccountable, as do the mysteries of culinary chemistry and philosophy that he has also taken note of. Spinoza's belief that *all reality* partakes in "the one substance that is everything [and] is infinitely self-causing, self-expressing, and self-sustaining [and which is] all-powerful, perfect, and real" (Dockstader) is a fitting transcendence for the artisan of tables and chairs, for the mender of damaged wickerwork.

These scraps of the father's "beliefs" are discovered after his death. The written words of the dead father, discovered when Rose is an adolescent, are unwelcome to her: "she pushed any discovery [about her father or Flo] aside with embarrassment and dread" (5), but they leave their trace as legacy, as proof of the existence of "another" father, one who carried out his life, his job, and his thoughts with "pride" and curiosity in an open relation to the mystery of being. Lacan suggests that "a woman can love in a man only the way in which he faces the knowledge thanks to which he souloves" (*SXX* 88), or in other words, for his "courage in bearing the intolerable relationship to the Supreme Being" (*SXX* 85). Whatever the Supreme Being may be for this father figure, his writings testify to a form of creative courage in the uniting of the everyday and the infinite, in bearing his mortality without losing "faith." That he is a simple man in a shack in Canada in the 1940s is irrelevant: "In each of us the path of the hero is traced, and it is precisely as an ordinary man that one follows it to the end" (*S VII* 393). This is the loved face of the father, idealized and cherished for what he represents beyond himself, or perhaps, for his holding open the sublime possibility of a "beyond oneself."

The Father's Law

The symbolic father, on the other hand, is the bearer of the neutrality of the law; as such, no particular person *is* this symbolic father; rather, it is a space within the social order that needs to be filled, necessarily imperfectly, by some figure who will take on the role, who will carry the burden of giving flesh to the paternal metaphor that guarantees social cohesion. This figure is called upon by Flo when "she and Rose can carry this [the bickering and recriminations] no further, by themselves" (16). Called out of the shed to mediate between Flo and Rose, to break the deadlock of their rivalry, the father is to expected to be both judge and enforcer of the law. Plainly, this is not a role this particular father-subject incarnates comfortably. While in fairy tales, the wicked stepmother often finds a woodsman, hunter, or some other emissary to carry out her jealous revenge, disguising and thereby preserving the "good" father, here the father is exposed in his punishing function. It is rather unwillingly that Rose's father steps in and assumes it: "He is slow at getting into the spirit of things, tired in advance, maybe, on the verge of rejecting the role he has to play" (17).

The first requirement of the role is to judge the status of Rose's transgression, which is unmistakably situated within the oedipal mother-daughter conflict. It is at this point that the fairy tale structure receives a twist: the traditional scenario requires that the wicked stepmother dominate Cinderella and make her work, whereby Cinderella becomes an oppressed figure who arouses sympathy in the reader. In "Royal Beatings," Cinderella has already got too big for her boots: Rose "sits on the kitchen table" while Flo "crawls underneath, scrubbing with the brush" (15). The frustration of the constraints of work, of life and its unfulfilled dreams, provokes Flo's irritation, and Rose becomes the designated target, all the more so as she remains untouched by Flo's ritual anger. To Flo's accusation that in spite of having "sacrificed her life" (15) for her, Rose "never [has] a thought for what [she's] doing" (16), Rose replies: "I never asked you to do anything. I wish you never had. I would have been a lot better off" (16). The scene gives us the disorder of adolescent rebellion, whereby the parent is challenged in her authority, negated in her symbolic place, and thereby humiliated. The fact that Rose is seated in a position above Flo gives spatial emphasis to her defiance. By making felt her growing detachment from the power of the (m)Other, by attempting to rid herself of the overwhelming power mothers wield in early childhood, Rose is fighting to gain her autonomy as a subject, but Flo is not to be so easily defeated. Thus, the dispute is perceived as one of many moments in a long struggle between them. Destructively fusional, the emotional struggle requires a mediator to end it, but to end it in such a way as to allow the mother to save face, since she cannot be defeated without symbolic confusion ensuing. What would it mean for the father to endorse the humiliation of the mother? The moment of judgment is therefore one of deep anxiety for Rose and, in a sense, nothing can go well from that point on: either the father reestablishes order by punishing her, or the father fails to reestablish order and the whole symbolic structure that allots a subjective position to each of them comes under threat. It is precisely this threat of the abolition of order, of place, of self that "leers" up with "malice" at Rose from the "patterns of linoleum" (19).

WORN PATTERNS: THE LINOLEUM GAZE

Linoleum is a common thing, but it is an odd word. Falsely reminiscent of words of Greek origin, it is made from flax (linum) and oil (oleum), and was a cheap and versatile floor covering commonly used up until 1950. Yet this is hardly a fact to explain the omnipresence of references to linoleum in the work of Munro: at one point in my reading, I started keeping a list of references to linoleum in the stories, but gave up, there were so many. The most famous reference, arguably the most oft-quoted passage from Munro's whole oeuvre, is from the end of the collection *Lives of Girls and Women:* "People's lives were dull, simple, amazing and unfathomable – deep caves paved with kitchen linoleum" (Munro, "Epilogue" 276).[6] The easily graspable construction of the depth / surface opposition, placed within the sphere of the everyday, and indeed, within the traditionally feminine, is a productive image that has led critics to emphasize the opposition between the banal and the mysterious, or between nature and culture.[7]

Most often, however, one does not need to look beneath Munro's linoleum to encounter the extraordinary: it is enough to look at it directly, for there is always something askew about it. It is that part of the decor that, in spite of being exactly in its place, somehow does not blend in; it nags at your peripheral vision and signals something worrying. In this sense, Munro's linoleum has something uncanny about it, something of the Lacanian gaze: "While it is always met with among objects, is always 'manifested in connection with the appearance of a sensible form,' which can be seen (in the slight parting of curtains on a window in a horror film, for example), or heard (the creaking of a door), or smelled (an exotic perfume), the gaze itself would swiftly evaporate were any of these sensible disturbances to become the index of a determinate observer, that is, were the Other of the gaze to become a determinate person, a small other" (Copjec, *Imagine* 210). The gaze is thus a subjective reading of the physical environment such that "dumb things" become heavy with menace. When this gaze appears, it is an index of anxiety: "what I apprehend … through these experiences of the gaze is not that '*there is someone there*; it is that I am vulnerable, that I have a body which can be hurt'" (Copjec, *Imagine* 211; inner quotation Sartre 347). As such, it is a subjective premonition of a threat of dissolution.

Most openly menacing just prior to Rose's beating, the linoleum gaze (extended to faded carpeting and other floor marks) is already surreptitiously at work early in the story. When Rose is accused of schooling her brother in vulgarity – "Yes, and that filth you taught to Brian" (13) – we read: "There is one step down from the kitchen to the woodshed, a bit of carpet on it so worn Rose can't ever remember seeing the pattern. Brian loosens it, dragging a tin" (14). Indistinct patterns (and we might note this hole in Rose's memory here as well) are the hallmark of these sites of the gaze, and here, on the road that leads to the father's shed, the worn carpet lifts,[8] exposing the rent in meaning that lies in wait. In the buildup of tension, the linoleum is kept down, under Flo's vigorous brush, but the destructive potential of the gaze is transferred onto her scrubbing: "An abnormal energy, a violent disgust, is expressed in the chewing of the brush at the linoleum" (15). Then, when Flo leaves the kitchen and Rose is left alone to await the oncoming storm of violence, there is a lull, and the linoleum momentarily offers the hope of a possible restoration of order: "The kitchen floor has five or six different patterns of linoleum on it. Ends, which Flo got for nothing and ingeniously trimmed and fitted together, bordering them with tin strips and tacks. While Rose sits on the table waiting, she looks at the floor, at this satisfying arrangement of rectangles, triangles, some other shape whose name she is trying to remember" (16). Borders, satisfying arrangements, a way for things to fit together: the linoleum momentarily (deviously) offers this as a possible world view, suggesting that Flo is part of that possibility, perhaps even the designer of it. However, Rose's memory is lacking one of the signifiers to "name" it. Is this missing signifier another form of the gaze? The one piece that won't fall into place, menacing the coherence of the whole pattern? Whatever we call this index of anxiety – the gaze, the evil eye, the malicious outside of meaning – it shifts from one location to another, from sound to visual inscription. Rose first "hears Flo coming back" and then "hears her father come in" (16), and these footsteps, first heard, are then seen: "[Flo's] shoes have left marks on the clean wet part of the floor" (17). Then the linoleum is summoned again as a "daily witness," the representative of the benevolent social perspective that Flo has attempted to shut out by closing four doors behind her (17), but it is no use: "Pots can show malice, the patterns of linoleum can leer up at you, treachery is the other side of dailiness" (19).

Within the fantasy construction, the moment that is being approached is the testing of the paternal metaphor, the ultimate guarantor of the "neutral stature of the symbolic [order]" (Žižek, *Enjoy* 178). Paradoxically, what the gaze menaces the subject with is not the efficiency of the paternal law, but the threat of its inefficiency: the possibility that it might in fact be lacking. In some sense, all those involved in the family drama must collaborate in the effectiveness of the paternal metaphor by accepting the myth behind the man, by giving authority to the man who sustains the myth. They must believe in, or make believe in him, or even make him believe they believe in him, so as to guarantee the efficacy of his function, so that, just as, above, when Rose *knew* that it would be "terrible" (6) if her father knew that she had heard his lalangue wordplay, she intuitively *knows* that she must not communicate her awareness that his authority is, in fact, ungrounded: that he is a semblance of a father, a stand-in for a function that he can only incarnate, never *be*. But Rose does not manage to guard her knowledge about the father's empty seat of authority from him: "Rose detects in her father some objections to Flo's rhetoric, some embarrassment and reluctance. She is wrong, and ought to know she is wrong, in thinking that she can count on this. The fact that she knows about it, and he knows she knows, will not make things any better. He is beginning to warm up" (17). This revelation of knowledge has a triggering effect of shifting the father into a different register. In allowing him *to see that she sees* his lack of certainty and commitment to his symbolic role, Rose demotes the father from his neutral symbolic function and challenges him, forcing into plain view the dark underside of the law, where despotic jouissance reigns in the form of "the obscene, uncanny, shadowy double of the Name of the father" (Žižek, *Enjoy* 180).

THE UNBRIDLED FATHER

The father, in punishing Rose, is therefore punishing her for two things: for "humiliating" Flo, but also for humiliating him, for unmasking his fundamental lack of authority as the father. In attempting to rectify this, he steps beyond the limits of the symbolic law he is supposed to uphold and provokes the wavering of the symbolic order. In that sense, he worsens the situation: a father who needs to beat a child to assure his authority becomes the perverted father (*père-version*), or as Fink puts it, "the unbridled father" (*A Clinical Introduction* 99),[9] acting not on behalf of the symbolic law but as the exception to it: "He gives her a look … It informs her of the hopelessness of her position. Then it clears, it begins to fill up with something else, the way a spring fills up when you clear the leaves away. It fills with hatred and pleasure" (18). Where the law sustains desire (by forbidding certain things) and guarantees the symbolic pact, the absence of law allows free reign to the drives, to tyrannical jouissance. This unfettering of the drives is metaphorically rendered in fluid terms, associating the law with the "leaves" that dam the spring of drives. The limits between the father in his paternal function and the licentious father are tenuous ones. Here, he uses a belt to beat her, and surprisingly, this can be understood as a metonym of the symbolic law: referring to a study by Niederland, Leader affirms that "the blows [in reported clinical fantasy accounts] [give] form to acoustic force, to the voice, an auditory presence linked to the father: what strikes the child may well be an empirical object like a whip, but this object is serving to embody the symbolic dimension of language" (Leader 110). Indeed, the "belt is coming off, not hastily. It is being grasped at the necessary point. *All right you*" (18). A semblance of control and of measure in the meting out of punishment characterizes the action and the words of the father at this point. But within minutes, Rose's resistance to being "belted" pushes the father outside his symbolic role: "Her father is after her, cracking the belt at her when he can, then *abandoning it and using his hands*" (19, my emphasis). Beyond that point, he is no longer constrained by the limits of the symbolic, but has slipped into the grotesque, the literary form of representation of the amoral drives. In this sense, unsupported by the law, both the father and Rose are torn out of the symbolic weave of family relationships, caught in a violent struggle for being: two Vancouvers fighting it out.

As dramatic as the situation is, it is not written as tragedy. In fact, it is in the conjoined violence of the beating and in the clear jubilatory tone of the telling that this incident signals itself as fantasy. There is pleasure in the father, as Rose sees him, but there is also enjoyment on Rose's part. Indeed, as a situation that corresponds for Rose to the statement "I am being beaten by my father," it enacts the second phase of the Freudian child-beating fantasy structure.[10] This phase "is identified unambiguously with a fantasy [and] is accompanied by a high yield of pleasure" (Leader 110).

Distanced only slightly through the use of the third person narrator, the beating is made emphatic through its auditory effects: "As [Niederland] points out, there is a 'close relation and possible interchangeability of sound and beating,' suggested linguistically by such terms as *beat*, *strike*, *blow*, *bang* and *hit*" (Leader 110). Indeed, the passage is marked by the repetitive use of "Bang": "Bang over the ear, then bang over the other ear. Back and forth, her head ringing. Bang in the face. Up against the wall and bang in the face again" (19). Rose is fully present throughout, not as a fading victim, whimpering and on the point of annihilation, but as a vigorous participant: "She draws back … She runs … she screams, she implores. She is incoherent, insane, shrieking. *Forgive me! Oh please, forgive me!*" (19). Only active verbal forms are used here such that the excessive dramatization of the scene and formalization of the language (*Forgive me!* rather than "I'm sorry") signal its status as scenario, as fantasy.

The acting metaphor is first introduced in relation to Rose's father, who is "quite out of character": "He is like a bad actor, who turns his part grotesque … That is not to say he is pretending, that he is acting, and does not mean it. He is acting, and he means it" (18). And the narrator attributes a similar theatricality to Rose: "for it seems Rose must play her part in this with the same grossness, the same exaggeration, that her father displays, playing his. She plays his victim with a self-indulgence that arouses, and maybe hopes to arouse, his final, sickened contempt" (19).[11] This theatricality gives fictional form to the familial structures that, in turn, give shape to what would otherwise be arbitrary subjective relationships: what, after all is a "father" to justify his punishment of a child? Family structures are beliefs that make up for the absence of a given structure of relationships, and belief in these structures "in so far as they are repressed … form[s] a constituent part of our ideological 'normality'" (Žižek, "Is There a Cause" 94). The idea that this is acting can only be formulated thanks to a slight inner distance that opens up in the perceiving narrator between her belief in the necessity of family roles, without which we would fall into a void of nonsignification, and her simultaneous nonbelief in the necessity of *this* role, *this* structure, *this* way.

The fantasy element in this scene in "Royal Beatings" may best be understood by comparing it with another version of the same moment to be found in the story-memoir "Fathers," where it receives a more directly expressed, personally engaged, first-person treatment that is quite impossible to read as fantasy. Munro recounts:

> My father had beaten me … Three or four times when I was around eleven or twelve … I was being punished at those times for some falling-out with my mother, some back talk or smart talk or intransigence. She would fetch my father from his outside work to deal with me, and I would await his arrival, first in balked fury, and then in sickening despair. I felt as if it must be my very self that they were after, and in a way I think it was. The self-important disputatious part of my self that had to be beaten out of me. When my father began to remove his belt – that was what he beat me with – I would begin to scream No, No, and plead my case incoherently, in a way that seemed to make him despise me. And indeed my behaviour then would arouse contempt, it did not show a proud or even a self-respecting nature. I did not care. And when the belt was raised – in the second before it descended – there was a moment of terrible revelation. Injustice ruled. I could never tell my side of things, my father's detestation of me was supreme. How could I not find myself howling at such perversion in nature? ("Fathers," *The View* 194–5)

Identical in almost every point of detail to the passage in "Royal Beatings" – the argument with the mother, the mother fetching the father from outdoors, the waiting, the belt, the screaming, the detestation and the very words "arouse contempt" are all there – this passage is nonetheless entirely different in tone. The first-person memoir style, the reference to the habitual or at least repeated aspect of the beatings, the fury and despair and injustice so vividly evoked in the remembering, the general breakdown of order and the feeling of having one's self submitted to "perversion in nature," all of this draws the reader into immediate empathy with the author / narrator and raises questions that sociological perspectives (What values in society supported this ritual punishment?) might enlighten but not exhaust the meaning of.

Indeed, what intrigues, finally, is what it meant to the girl: both in the distanced fantasy version and in the painfully remembered memoir version, the telling bears witness to the desire to be loved by the father. In the fantasy, the beating constitutes a veiling of the libidinal excitement of the real and is related to parental desire, as we shall see in the following section, whereas in the memoir version, the episode ends on a plea for reinstatement within the idealized sphere of the "good" father: "He was a man of honor and competence and humor, and he was the parent I sorely wanted to please" ("Fathers," *View* 195). Although the memory is clearly painful, the perspective is not one of judgment of the father but, surprisingly, of the self: "I did not hate him, could not consider hating him. Instead, I saw what he hated in me. A shaky arrogance in my nature, something brazen yet cowardly, that woke in him this fury" (195). This is followed by an astonishing conclusion where the word *shame* is hammered down four times, reinforced by the words *beaten* and *beating*: "Shame. The shame of being beaten, and the shame of cringing from the beating. Perpetual shame. Exposure" (195). It is, structurally, a retelling of the same story, but the force or perhaps the direction of the affect is different: emphatic and yet theatrically distanced in "Royal Beatings," the emotional impact of the violence is brought more sharply into view in "Fathers." In both versions, the story moves from the violence of the beatings, to a feeling that one's very self is being fought (over), to the shame that follows. I will now return to "Royal Beatings" to consider these last two aspects: the self at stake, and the shame that, in this fantasy version, goes by the name of humiliation.

THE FUNDAMENTAL FANTASY

One way of accounting for Rose's wish to arouse her father's contempt is to see it in terms of the fundamental fantasy. In Lacanian theory, the subject's symbolic consistency is guaranteed by a fundamental fantasy that gives her support for her being in the world, for the inconceivable *fact of being* and the immense complexity of finding one's place in the sphere of the desire of the Other: "What fantasy stages is precisely the subject's impossible being [which is] lost owing to the subject's entry into the symbolic order. No wonder, then, that the fundamental fantasy is passive, 'masochistic,' reducing me to an object acted upon by others: it is as if only the experience of the utmost pain can guarantee the subject access to Being: *la douleur d'exister* means that I 'am' only in so far as I experience pain" (Žižek, "Is It Possible to Traverse" 119). While the potential necessity of confronting pain in the process of subjectification may seem unpalatable, it is essential to keep in mind that fantasy is not transposable as the teleological object of an actual wish or desire: it is not the response to the question *What do I want?* but rather, *What do they want of me?* As fundamental fantasy, it is an unconscious configuration of the subject's personal myth of being. The basic principle of the fundamental fantasy is precisely that the subject *refuses* it: it is not a view of the self that the self adheres to consciously. In this context, we could see Rose's "wish" to arouse contempt in her father as a fantasized version of her need to test the very existence of her being through the pain of being reduced to an object, an object that could be destroyed. Stated differently, the function of the fantasy here is to interpret the desire of the Other, to discover where / how the Other is lacking. In response to this lack in the Other (Flo's lack of authority, for example), the child offers her own fundamental lack: the *beinglessness* that was the subject's "first guise." In other words, she provokes the question: *Do they want me to disappear?*: "The first object [the child] proposes for this parental desire whose object is unknown is his loss – *Does he want to lose me*? The phantasy of one's death, of one's disappearance, is the first object that the subject has to bring into play in this dialectic, and he does indeed bring it into play – as we know from innumerable cases, such as in anorexia nervosa. We also know that the phantasy of one's death is usually manipulated by the child in his love relations with his parents" (Lacan, *SXI* 214–15).[12] Rose does not attempt to escape her beating – she does not leave the kitchen, does not apologize for being insolent, or use any of the many strategies children employ to avoid punishment – she seems to consider the beating inevitable. She sits and waits, and then lets it play out.

She will finally be reassured by the "restraint" in the father's kicks, and by Flo "shrieking … *Stop, stop!*" (19). The threat of self-annihilation is thwarted, and Rose can enjoy its jouissance potential a while longer:

formulations of other forms of disappearance invade her thoughts, always in dialectic with parental response. She is certain that she will "never forgive them. She will punish them; she will finish them. Encased in these finalities, and in her bodily pain, she floats in curious comfort, beyond herself, beyond responsibility. Suppose she dies now? Suppose she commits suicide? … She floats in her pure superior state as if kindly drugged" (20). Hate and love become entangled in the extremity of a situation where one is beaten for "one's own good," where anger against the parents is inseparable from dependency on their love, where the movement toward autonomy from the parental sphere provokes a humiliating regression of the self to the status of parental object. Thus these offers to disappear, to "commit suicide," are aggressively directed at the parents: the fantasy involves its component of revenge. Through this process, Rose imagines that she is now "superior" to her parents, that she has secured her autonomy of being, even the right to dispose of herself, and that her parents can no longer attain her.

But this is not the end of it. Desire is fundamentally inscribed within the symbolic order and its dependency on the law; Flo is, in this case, the agent who *invokes* the law, by calling in the father, and she is also the agent of the normalization of the symbolic order after the beating. She offers Rose the means to return "to the family" and assures her that her place within parental affection has not been annihilated by the collective outburst of violence. Yet with this return into the realm of the Other's desire comes the fall: the fall from the "curious comfort" and from the sense of being "beyond responsibility." The return of love includes being subjected anew to the desire of the Other; for Rose, this resubjection to the "mother's" desire passes through and is tarred with humiliation. It is humiliation that gives Rose the answer to the question *What do they want of me?* And more specifically, *What does my "mother" want?*

THE WICKED STEPMOTHER

Indeed, Flo's role in the beating scenario is crucial: her words open the short story in the form of a prophecy: "*Royal Beating.* That was Flo's promise. You are going to get one Royal Beating" (3). Later, she gives the beating its raison d'être: "'She humiliates me,' she says, straightening up. There it is, the explanation. 'She humiliates me,' she repeats with satisfaction" (17).

An uneasy spectator to the violence she has set in motion, Flo moves in once it is finished and orchestrates the return to normalcy, which requires not simply that Rose be beaten, but that Rose be humiliated. Earlier, I noted that the anxiety of the gaze is related to the fact that one has a body that can be hurt; it can also signal shame, stripping away all that covers over the intimacy of our being. Hearing Flo's "step on the stairs" (20) is another manifestation, an aural one, of the "gaze" that announces both the return of the symbolic and its threats and menaces: it announces the "moment in which you know the whole protection has fatally cracked" when Rose is faced with the "sure knowledge of the whole down-spiraling course of events" (20).

Flo brings Rose a pot of humiliation in the form of "cold cream. Rose can smell it. The intimate, babyish, humiliating smell. She won't allow it near her. But in order to avoid it, the big ready clot of it in Flo's hand, she has to move. She scuffles, resists, loses dignity" (21). The clot of cold cream slides metonymically into the "overflow" of food temptations: chocolate milk, butter tarts, sandwiches spilling over with filling, all this arouses Rose's appetite and leaves her "miserably tempted, roused and troubled and drawn back from thoughts of suicide or flight by the smell of salmon ... soon, in helpless corruption, she will eat them all ... though she sniffles with shame. Too late" (21). By giving in to her appetites, she reaffirms Flo's knowledge of her secret desires, and Flo's power to manipulate and shape them, and by the same gesture, reaffirms Flo's place as Queen of the Royal Beatings; in allowing herself to be humiliated twice by Flo, once as the object of an orchestrated beating whereby she offers her nonexistence as a possibility, and second as the manipulable object of Flo's desire, willing to accept humiliation as the sacrifice for love, Rose temporarily secures her place within the maternal affections.

THE BEYOND OF FANTASY

There is a cost for the subject's participation in the desire of the Other, a resentment that emerges from a possible slippage: from trying to "plug up" the lack in the Other by offering one's own lack, to the suspicion of being made the object or plaything of the Other's jouissance.

Rose works out this resentment in two opposite directions. First, by offering an "it could be worse" beating scenario, through the extended rumour / legend / local story / anecdote about Becky Tyde, a motherless, polio-stricken child who is beaten, but also rumoured to have been raped, impregnated by her butcher father, who then "disposed of" the baby. Mr Tyde is seen primarily as an avatar of the tyrannical father of the mythical primal horde who must therefore be killed by the "sons," that is, the local vigilante townsmen who "meant to hold a mock trial but ... could not remember how it was done. So they began to beat him and kept beating him until he fell" (10). He dies in the aftermath of the beating. This story-within-the-story points to the crossing of a limit: "there is a *threshold* of sorts within fantasy itself, the point beyond which it turns to horror; ... when suddenly what we most ardently desire turns out to be something else altogether, something absolutely horrible. The purity of desire veers in the direction of a kind of *obscene jouissance*" (Fink, *A Clinical Introduction* 129). As for Becky, with her mother already dead, the father having been killed, and the law circumvented, there is no simple way for her to reintegrate a place in the symbolic system; she survives the violence, but there is no return to a subjective place within any dialectic of desire. Since the desire for parental love that Rose is finally reassured of is not given to Becky Tyde, she is a victim who remains stuck in the phase of "superiority" that Rose evoked, in the aftermath of violence and before the return to "normalcy," but that place above is also "outside." She is fixed in the position of the beaten object, a grotesquely embodied vision or version of the drives: "a big-headed, loud-voiced dwarf, with a mascot's sexless swagger" (8); half-cartoon, neuter, indulging her oral pleasure: "She would put a whole cookie in her mouth if she felt like it, let her cheeks puff out like a frog's" (8). The structure of Becky's rumoured fate is not without similarity to Rose's story, but everything is exaggerated and excessive; in the Becky Tyde story, the script moves toward the "*obscene jouissance*" that signals the "beyond" of Rose's fantasy.[13]

In Rose's case, where fantasy remains on the near side of that threshold and includes "some restraint" (19), the beating is but a momentary rent in the fabric of the symbolic order, which quickly resumes its consistency: "they will all sit around the table eating again, listening to the radio news ... They will be embarrassed, but rather less than you might expect" (21). This embarrassment is, in itself, the trace of the reestablishment of the social. As a variation on shame, the communal embarrassment is a form of acknowledgement of the lack in the Other, so that the "convalescent indolence," "satisfaction," "relaxation, even a current of happiness" that pervades the post-beating moment, aside from the postcoital connotations that Carrington points out (45), may also signal relief that the social pact as such has not been definitively blown apart.

The second way in which Rose's resentment toward the mother for her overpowering desire is carried out is through a reduction of the mother to the drive itself; the final image of the story sees both Flo and Hat Nettleton, one of the village vigilantes who "punished" Mr Tyde, placed in the local retirement home. Hat Nettleton is already dead at the moment being referred to, but his voice emerges from the radio in Rose's kitchen "many years later" (22), a disembodied voice from the past, a partial object of the drives, delectating in the vulgarity permitted to the very old: "Some [work horses ...] pull till they drop down dead and some wouldn pull your cock out of a pail of lard. Hehe" (23). As for Flo, her voice is silent: "After Rose put her in the Home ... she had stopped talking. She had removed herself, and spent most of her time sitting in a corner of her crib, looking crafty and disagreeable, not answering anybody, though she occasionally showed her feelings by biting a nurse" (24). The humiliation undergone by Rose, "babied" with cold cream, now alights on Flo, who is removed from proximity with the father, is confined, like a baby, to a crib, and stripped of language, she reverts to primal oral aggression – biting – to express herself. One dead, the other dying, both now outside of language, Flo and Hat Nettleton are reduced to a couple of pickled arseholes, nonsensical signifiers. Pure revenge fantasy: the stepmother, by fairy tale definition necessarily "wicked," gets her just deserts.

"Princess Ida"

Sublimation, Repression, and the Return of the Repressed

In contrast to the "wicked stepmother" side of the maternal figure seen in "Royal Beatings," "Princess Ida" focuses on the mother in her own right as an autonomous subject, and situates her in relation to her *own* mother. This shifting of generational perspective produces a more empathetic narrative, where the focalizing child, named Del, attempts to understand her mother and to decode her through the enigmatic signs that are attributed to her.

"THE PROBLEM, THE ONLY PROBLEM IS MY MOTHER"

The centrality of the mother figure in an interconnecting web of Munro's stories has been pointed out in several critical works, notably by Ferri, Heller, and Thacker ("Introduction"). Taken collectively, these critics address the autobiographical details of Munro's own mother, Anne Clarke Laidlaw (née Chamney), and the progressive deterioration of her health due to the effects of her tardily diagnosed Parkinson's disease; they have noted that the stories that draw on this source illustrate the need to both love the mother and reject the debased maternal image – "Our Gothic Mother" as she is described by the narrator's sister in "The Peace of Utrecht" (*Dance* 195). They have also pointed toward the ongoing revisions of the mother figure that continues to haunt Munro's stories in collection after collection, much as the narrator in "The Ottawa Valley" foresees her mother will: "The problem, the only problem is my mother … she has stuck to me as close as ever and refused to fall away, and I could go on, and on, applying what skills I have, using what tricks I know, and it would always be the same" (*Something* 197).

Surprisingly, "Princess Ida" has not generally been acknowledged in critical studies as a key mother-figure story, perhaps in part because *Lives of Girls and Women* was officially published as a novel. Its parts were therefore seen as indissociable: Munro, however, acknowledges quite directly that although her intention was indeed to write a novel, what she actually produced was something different:

> I went up to the office and started to write the section called "Princess Ida," which is about my mother. The material about my mother is my central material in life, and it always comes the most readily to me. If I just relax, that's what will come up. So, once I started to write that, I was off. Then I made a big mistake. I tried to make it a regular novel, an ordinary sort of childhood adolescence novel. About March I saw it wasn't working. It didn't feel right to me, and I thought I would have to abandon it. I was very depressed. Then it came to me that what I had to do was pull it apart and put it in the story form. Then I could handle it. That's when I learned that I was never going to write a real novel because I could not think that way. (McCulloch and Simpson)[1]

Here, both the centrality of "Princess Ida" as a key mother-figure text in Munro's writing and the nonconformity of *Lives of Girls and Women* to the standard criteria of the novel form are acknowledged. In recent criticism, a general shift toward a recognition of the book's identity as a "story sequence," or set of "interlinked stories" (Beer), has taken place.

Nonetheless, "Princess Ida" has generally been left out of recent discussions of what are considered to be Munro's mother-figure stories. Robert Thacker categorizes some of these as "offer[ing] a type of 'family resemblance' born of their autobiographical provenance." He notes in passing that this figure appears "emotionally if not precisely – in *Lives of Girls and Women* as Ida" ("Introduction" 14), a lapsus whereby part of the character's pen name, Princess Ida, stands in place of her actual identity as Ada / Addie in the story.[2] Heller and Ferri both point to a series of mother-daughter stories including "The Peace of Utrecht" (*Dance*), "The Ottawa Valley" (*Something*),

"The Progress of Love" (*Progress*), and "Friend of My Youth" (*Friend*), but do not list "Princess Ida" among them.[3] My perspective here will be to consider "Princess Ida" as the first *story* fully and specifically focused on the mother figure. Momentarily, in the scope of Munro's writing, the figure of the sick, bed-ridden, or dead mother present in *Dance of the Happy Shades* is left aside: in "Princess Ida," the mother is restored to a greater complexity, even if, in the final stories of *Lives of Girls and Women*, she is relegated to her bed once again ("Baptizing" 253, 263).

In her book-length study of mother figures in Munro, *Mothers and Other Clowns,* Magdalene Redekop focuses briefly on "Princess Ida," pointing out the echoing interplay of Ida / Ada / Addie / Adelaide / Del and relating these to the Tennysonian intertext, as well as to Faulkner's Addie in *As I Lay Dying* and to Nabokov's Ada in *Ada or Ardor: A Family Chronicle.* What is of more relevance to my argument here is that Redekop qualifies "Princess Ida" as "the uterus out of which is born not one perfect baby or one novel but multiple offspring" and as "the place of origins," a "place that *cannot be seen or represented*" (65, my emphasis). Consequently, Redekop moves on to other stories in *Lives of Girls and Women.*

While I would agree that "Princess Ida" is a story of origins, I would also argue that the text does indeed offer ways to approach the obscurity of its meaning: ways which do not clarify the hypothetical "conscious blind spot" that Redekop posits (65), but which acknowledge the workings of the unconscious in the text. There is in "Princess Ida," as in the later, similarly structured story "The Progress of Love," "a cloud, a poison, that had touched [the] mother's life" (*Progress* 17).[4] This cloud, the mother's burden, is rooted somewhere in the past in "Princess Ida," a past shaped by economic, cultural, and affective poverty and that includes sexual abuse, religious fanaticism, and patriarchal domination. But there is also courage, determination, and the hope of social advancement. Resentful and triumphant, the voice of Del's mother speaks of repressed pain and sublimated objects of culture, and in its negations, its excesses, its irony and chosen images, the story enacts the working of the language of the unconscious and its irruptions into the discourses of everyday life. By following the narrating daughter's desire to understand her mother, and by also turning our attention to the mother's replies, memories, and actions, we return not so much to a fruitful uterus as to a hard core of hurt, which produces effects that can indeed be seen and represented.

As the narrating voice that accounts for her mother's story, Del is split between the child's naïve perspective and that of the more reflective, remembering adult she has become, in "a commingling of the remembered event, vividly described so as to lend immediacy to it, and [a] detached understanding of it, an understanding that is detached because of the time which has passed" (Thacker, "Clear Jelly" 45). Thus, Del, in "Princess Ida," is both the preadolescent girl still partially in the thrall of the all-powerful mother of early childhood, but nevertheless beginning the process of adolescent self-differentiation, *and* the adult narrator trying to use the perspective of time to reevaluate both her mother and her own expectations of that mother.

This intricate weaving of levels of closeness and detachment is present from the start of the story, and coheres around the mother's enthusiasm for selling encyclopedias.[5] For Del's mother, knowledge "was not chilly …, no; it was warm and lovely," and this passion is also her daughter's: "I shared my mother's appetite myself, I could not help it. I loved the volumes of the encyclopedia, their weight (of mystery, of beautiful information) as they fell open in my lap" (74). There is something almost sensual in this love of knowledge for Del, who wonders, "And who could fail to love me, for knowing where Quito was?" (75). It is when she realizes that she is *not* loved for such knowledge, that it is not valued in her, or in her mother, by the community she belongs to, that Del detaches herself from the open display of her "freak memory" (75) and from the penchant for public display on her mother's part. Yet, in spite of her later self-distancing from her mother's activities, throughout this early period Del remains reluctantly enthralled with her mother: "Over all our expeditions, and homecomings, and the world at large, she exerted this mysterious, appalling authority, and nothing could be done about it, not yet" (77–8). The formulation of this perspective on her mother, with the oedipal rivalry of adolescence anticipated but not yet fully active, speaks of the child's admiration, but with a sophistication belonging to the adult voice.

THE MOTHER'S "GLOOM"

Within this realm of female identification, Del feels compelled to question her mother's desire in the field of affections. When her mother takes a rented house in town for the winter season, effectively disuniting the family, Del seeks reassurance that it is a practical and not an affective split: "I said to my mother, 'Why didn't you bring that picture in [from the other house]?' 'What picture? *What picture?*' 'The one over the couch'" (80). The picture in question is one that Del's mother had painted some time ago, showing "sheep driven along the road by a little girl in a red shawl" (80); Del has romanticized it into an original creation by an artistic mother, painted in early marriage, even believing that the girl in the picture was actually her mother. The mother has no such romantic notions: "'That one? Do you want that in here?' I didn't really. As often in our conversations I was trying to lead her on, to get the answer, or the revelation, I particularly wanted. I wanted her to say she had left it for my father" (80). Here, the narrator speaks of her need to see her mother in a certain light, to make her conform to a model of womanhood, of being, that she, Del, will then be able to take comfort in and identify with: the model of a woman who loves her husband. Also, as seen in the previous chapter, the question may be aiming at reassurance that her own arrival in the world was the product of love between her parents, and that her place in the world was marked out by their mutual desire for each other, and for her to be. But the answers her mother gives fall short of the child's expectations: "'I don't want it hanging where people would see,' she said. 'I'm no artist. I only painted it because I had nothing to do'" (81). The mother's answer is marked by negativity – "don't want," "no," "only," "nothing."

This question is the first in a series addressed to the mother in the same vein, which is to say, seeking to verify the mother's affections. In subsequent instances the questions become more direct and the answers more oblique, to the extent that the abrupt reply, "of course," will become a textual sign of the mother's refusal to go into sensitive areas. The first of these occurs when Del questions her mother about her relationship to her own mother, and her feelings after she died: "'Were you sad?' I said hopefully and my mother said yes, of course she was sad. But she did not linger around this scene" (87). Here, we note the rhythm of the formulation, where the mother's direct speech is worked into the narration, leaving no time for further questioning, no time to "linger" and expand or reflect. It is a minimalist answer intended to close down further discussion on the matter.

Moreover, this brisk reply contrasts with the expansive force of the negative anecdotes about her own mother that Del's mom recounts in detail, and which convey to her daughter a sense of gothic origins, an archetypal past located outside of rational time, somewhere in the fairy-tale temporality of the unconscious where "In the beginning, the very beginning of everything, there was that house" (83), a house that had "something terrible about it, enclosing evil, like a house where a murder has been committed" (84). If the house represents that place where we live, both psychologically and physically (Corelli), then Del's mother's representation of the house of her childhood speaks of oppression and moral disorder. Within that house lived the tyrannical father, who would later refuse to allow her to go to high school (87), but more importantly, the mother: "She was a religious fanatic," declares Del's mother, and adds, "'Do you know what she did? I told you what she did? I told you about the money?' She draws a breath to steady herself. 'Well. She inherited some money'" (85). Del's mother goes on to describe the unpardonable gesture of this mother of hers who spent the small inheritance she had been given on bibles to distribute to the poor, rather than on the basic necessities that could have alleviated the hardships suffered by her own, very poor, family. Remembered as unforgivably pious, and long-suffering, Del's grandmother lives on in her mother's memory as a source of pain and resentment: "My mother's voice, telling these things, is hard with her certainty of having been cheated, her undiminished feelings of loss and anger" (85). In this context, it is not a matter "of course" that Del's mother should have felt sad at the death of her own mother.

An even more sensitive issue for Del is her mother's relationship to romance, love, and sexuality. Del tries to trap her mother into affirming that her marriage was a marriage of love. This, in the context of Del's mother having rented a house in town while the father remains on their rural farm throughout the winter, is a subject of some pertinence; yet Del seems to hope, in spite of the clear independence and even distance between her parents, that there was, in the beginning, some passion, some intimate tenderness and affection. In a form that is only half-questioning, Del insists: "'But you fell in love with him' I would remind her sternly, anxiously, wanting to get it settled for good. 'You fell in love'" (89). As any other response to this question would require saying more than the mother wishes to reveal to her daughter, she replies, "Well yes of course I did." Here, as above, the lack of punctuation makes of this a rote answer. Del insists, "Why did you fall in love?" to which her mother replies, "Your father was always a gentleman." Del reflects, "Was that all? I was troubled here by a lack of proportion, though it was hard to say what was missing, what was wrong" (89). As a child, Del cannot penetrate beyond this deflecting response that her mother offers her.

However, from her position as narrating voice, the adult version of Del disseminates suggestions throughout the text that her mother's answer is symptomatic of her rejection of sexuality. In choosing to marry a "gentleman," Del's mother is indirectly pointing out her rejection of those men for whom sexuality is a dominant concern. Among these textual insinuations is the reference to a former suitor, a "young man who remained a shadow ... For mysterious reasons she was compelled to break her engagement. ('He did not turn out to be the sort of person I had thought he was.')" (89). References to the general rejection of sexuality on the part of Del's mother also punctuate the other stories in the collection: in "Lives of Girls and Women," she comments on the relationship between her boarder, Fern, and Mr Chamberlain: "'They enjoy each other's company,' she said. 'They don't bother about any nonsense.'" And the narrating voice comments: "Nonsense meant romance; it meant vulgarity; it meant sex" (162). In this way, the whole question of love and courtship is held together under the label of "vulgarity" for Del's mother. Why should this be so? The rejection of sexual desire on the part of Del's mother is inscribed as a *persistent* trace from her childhood, related to some form of sexual torment on the part of her brother. Again, this is stated through hints and allusions, but they are sufficiently clear for the reader to understand the force of their effect. In her bitter accounts of her youth, Del's mother refers to her detested brother:

> It was the younger brother she hated. What did he do? Her answers were not wholly satisfactory. He was evil, bloated, cruel. A cruel fat boy. He fed firecrackers to cats. He tied up a toad and chopped it to pieces. He drowned my mother's kitten, named Misty, in the cow trough, though he afterwards denied it. Also, he caught my mother and tied her up in the barn and tormented her. Tormented her? He *tortured* her.
>
> What with? But my mother would never go beyond that – that word, *tortured*, which she spat out like blood. So I was left to

> imagine her tied up in the barn, as at a stake, while her brother, a fat Indian, yelped and pranced about her. But she had escaped after all, unscalped, unburnt. Nothing really accounted for her darkened face at this point in the story, for her way of saying *tortured.* I had not yet learned to recognize the gloom that overcame her in the vicinity of sex. (86)

In her recounting of this passage, the narrator retains the unconscious deflecting strategies of her mother's discourse and simultaneously imprints the force of the unwelcome memories. The emotional intensity of the mother's hatred of her brother can be felt in the accumulation of adjectives attributed to him – "evil," "bloated," "cruel" (twice), "fat" – as well as in the thrice-italicized verb "*tortured.*" Similarly, an accumulation of displaced actions, close to, but differing from, the act inflicted upon the mother, allows the narrator to evoke her mother's anger without naming its cause: is it not enough that he tortured and killed small helpless animals such as kittens to be convinced of his intrinsic malevolence? Phrases such as "Her answers were *not* wholly satisfactory," "my mother would *never* go beyond that – that word," and "*Nothing* really accounted for her darkened face" (my emphasis) signal through their negations that the central traumatic event in the mother's memory cannot be named, leaving the child, Del, within the limits of her young imagination, to conjure up stereotypical enemies and child's play scenes of torture. Unconscious metonymy of meaning is at work in this conjuring: to make sense of her mother's incomplete narrative and of her "darkened face," Del displaces this notion of darkness onto a scenario where her mother may have been burnt, "as at a stake." This scenario, helped along through a mental image of the brother as "a fat Indian, [who] yelped and pranced about her" is simultaneously evoked and found wanting through the signifier "unburnt"; the narrator, as a child, can find no satisfactory explanation for her mother's somber countenance. Only later, as an adult, can she reinterpret her mother's silence; only later, once she has, in fact, "learned to recognize the gloom that overcame her [mother] in the vicinity of sex," can she fill in the unsaid of her mother's intense emotions. In this last phrase, the enigma of the mother's repressed anger is largely clarified: the metonymic chain can be followed through from "tied up," to "tormented," to "tortured," and finally to "the vicinity of sex."[6]

The childhood of Del's mother as a time of affective misery, with its emblematic unmentionable trauma, is reinforced by the textual markers presenting Del's grandmother as also having had an unhappy relationship to sexuality. Indeed, Del's maternal grandmother is remembered as a broken woman: "bent back, narrow shouldered in some gray or tan sweater over a dirty kimono or housedress, the back of the head with the thin hair pulled tight from the middle parting, the scalp unhealthily white. It was white as marble, white as soap" (84). This first image of Del's grandmother's "bent back" suggests her submissiveness, and her "gray, tan, dirty" clothes imply a lack of attention to her appearance. Her thinning hair exposes her "scalp," a signifier that picks up on the earlier "unscalped" attributed to Del's mother, and which, unlike "skin," is associated with death, the marble whiteness evoking the tombstone. The word "soap" suggests the cleanliness and, of course, the godliness that is her compensation for suffering. She is remembered "on her knees, bent down on the bed, praying," or at other times "is discovered flat on her back and weeping – for reasons my mother does not go into – with a damp cloth pressed to her forehead" (84–5). The central object in both of these memories is the bed, the symbol of marital sexuality, and the grandmother is seen either praying by it or crying on it.[7] We have already come to understand that the narrator, in saying "for reasons my mother does not go into," is inscribing the notion of unspeakable sexuality into her mother's discourse.

SUBLIMATION ...

The general inability of Del's mother to see sexuality as a dynamic, enriching, positive aspect of a woman's life is therefore rooted in specific subjective events of the past that are traceable in the text, in the enigmatic forms in which the narrator distills them. Both Del's mother and grandmother are marked by discourses of repression in relation to sexuality. Their life force and desires go elsewhere. They are both fanatics in that they pour the greater part of their psychical energy into one specified area: in the case of the grandmother, religion is the object of her love, whereas for the mother, knowledge is the elected field of devotion. Freud's well-known theory of sublimation posits the substitution of sexual objects by cultural aims: "Sublimation is a process that concerns object-libido [the energy directed towards an object] and consists in the instinct's directing itself towards an aim other than, and remote from, that of sexual satisfactions; in this process the accent falls upon deflection from sexuality" ("On Narcissism" 88). This formulation has led to the general understanding that sublimation involves a renouncement of sexual activity.

Lacan opposes this reading of Freud: "Sublimation is not, in fact, what the foolish crowd thinks; it does not on all occasions necessarily follow the path of the sublime. The change of object doesn't necessarily make the sexual object disappear – far from it; the sexual object acknowledged as such may come to light in sublimation" (*SVII* 198). Beyond this clarification, Lacan, in his lesson on "The Deconstruction of the Drive" (*SXI* 161–73), brings out a subtler perspective on sublimation: he notes that Freud conceptualizes the drive as "a constant force" (*SXI* 164)[8] whose object, from a theoretical perspective, is "*a matter of total indifference*" (*SXI* 168). Contrary to the idea that the drive is satisfied by attaining its object, Lacan's proposition is that sublimation consists in circling round the object, which is not an object per se, but something that functions as objet a, the cause of desire. The sublimated object is therefore an object that has taken on subjective value as "that which causes me to desire."

... AND ITS OBJECTS

There is no necessity, therefore, to oppose sexuality and other passion-producing pursuits; love, art, religion, collecting, or politics may all involve objects raised, in the subject's perspective, "to the dignity of the Thing" (Lacan, *SVII* 138). Moreover, the drive, distinct from animal instinct, is a characteristic of the *speaking* subject, and is not without a relation to the symbolic order and the social bond. The drive is not satisfied by the *satisfaction* of a need, because the demand that carries it "always under- or overshoots itself; ... because it articulates itself through the signifier, it always demands something else" and involves a relation to the Other, to socially recognized discourses: "It is after all as a function of the problem of ethics that we have to judge sublimation; it creates socially recognized values" (Halpern). In a context where their experience of sexuality has complicated their relationship to genital love, both Del's mother and grandmother have found other objects, the socially valued spheres of knowledge and religion, around which to positively expend the "constant force" of their libidinal drive, and thereby hang on to their potential for desire, or as Bruce Fink names it, their *desirousness*.[9]

Religion is indeed the affective centre of Del's grandmother's life, as witnessed not only by the details given above but also, later in the story, by way of an anecdote offered by Del's Uncle Bill, her mother's hated brother. He remembers their mother directing their attention to the transformation of a chrysalis into a butterfly, emphasizing the symbolic importance of it happening on Easter day. With the exception of this example, all the information relating to this devoutly Christian woman is filtered through the resentment of Del's mother: thinking back to the inscription on the emblematic bibles – "Blessed are the poor in spirit" – she snorts, "What is so remarkable about being poor in spirit?" (85); concerning her enforced enrolment in bible distribution, she notes, "One thing, it cured me of religion for life" (85).

"Cured" of religion, finding no enjoyment in the contemplation or the anticipation of sexuality, Del's mother is not without desire: for her, knowledge, learning, education, and cultural pursuits become her passionate objects. From the opening line of the story – "Now my mother was selling encyclopedias" (72) – to her triumphant battle to go to high school, in spite of her father's refusal (87–8), on through the intertextual reference to Tennyson's "Princess" in her choice of pen name, to her writing of letters to the local newspaper and her joining the "Great Books discussion group" (82), the story tells us unconditionally that Ada is in love with knowledge: "Pure comfort even at this stage of her life to know where the location of the Celebes Sea and the Pitti Palace, to get the wives of Henry VIII in order, and be informed about the social system of ants, the methods of sacrificial butchery used by the Aztecs, the plumbing in Knossos. She could get carried away, telling about such things" (74). The narrator develops the portrait of her knowledge-hungry mother in ways that verge on the absurd, emphasizing how her excessiveness makes her an outsider in their community. As noted earlier, Del understands this pleasure of the intellect and finds it tempting herself, but refuses to give it exclusivity.

THE RETURN OF THE REPRESSED

The crux of the story, linking repression, sublimation, and an attempt to make one's peace with who one has become, comes in the last section with the return of the repressed in the form of an unexpected visit from the hated brother, now a tall, heavy American: "mournful, proud, sagging" (91), accompanied by an improbable femme fatale, his young wife named Nile. His status as an intruder, as someone who oversteps his rights, is signalled in the description of his approach. The narrator remembers herself as a child, outdoors: "I saw a big car come nosing along between the snowbanks almost silently, like an impudent fish" (91). Here, Munro's use of simile works very effectively, transforming the car moving slowly through the liquid world of snow into the phallic shape of a fish, insolent and unquestioning in its pushy advance. The transformation of "Bill" into an American underlines this sense of territorial expansion of the strong over the weak.[10]

For Del's mother, metaphorically, this is the visit of the torturer to his victim, the intrusion of the past source of her still active anger into her present, the signifier of her signified: that of a robbed innocence. Interestingly, Freud notes that the repressed behaves like an unwelcome guest attempting to cross the threshold into consciousness: "I must set a permanent guard over the door which I have forbidden this guest to enter, since he would otherwise burst it open" ("Repression" 152–3). Through his fish-like, unannounced approach, Bill slips into his sister's home.

In her typical style of deflection and affirmation of negatives, Del's mother greets her unwelcome visitor with a social veneer of welcome over a thinly disguised rejection: "'Well, Bill. You don't believe in advance notice, do you? Never mind, we're happy to see you.' She said this with some severity, as if arguing a point" (92). The visit is a study in misrecognition, where Bill attempts to share with his sister memories of a childhood that he cherishes, with their mother as the saintly centre of a shining past: "We had a simple life and hard work and fresh air and a good spiritual example in our momma. She died young, Addie. She died in pain." Resentful of what she sees as an attempt to embellish the past, Del's mother will not concede a thing: "Under anesthetic," my mother said. "So strictly speaking I hope she did not die in pain" (97).

There will be no moment of reconciliation between brother and sister.[11] Whether the brother has forgotten, forgiven himself, or never even registered any sense of guilt toward his sister, for her, resentment remains intact and non-negotiable. From the perspective of Del, it is difficult to reconcile the force of her mother's anger with the innocuous man she sees before her. She tries in vain to find traces of her mother's former tormentor but cannot detect the "cruel fat boy" in this newly discovered uncle: "He was gone, smothered, like a little spotted snake, once venomous and sportive, buried in a bag of meal" (98–9). Troubled by this discrepancy, she inquires of her mother: "Do you still hate him?" and her mother is forced into her third instance of a negatively formulated affirmation: "'Of course I don't hate him,' said my mother quickly and with reserve" (101). Of the three instances of "of course" that we have seen, this one most transparently allows its contradictory force to speak out: the affirmative "of course" comes up against a negative, which is not followed up by any affirmative statement of affect.

LIFTING THE REPRESSION, "LIKE THE DOWNFLASH OF A WING OR KNIFE"

Del's mother is thus faced with a dilemma when, on departing, her brother tells her that he has cancer, that he is dying, and that he is going to leave her three hundred dollars in his will. This gift from the brother she hated reactivates both her resentment toward him and the previous hurt related to her own mother's (mis)use of her inheritance. She tries to evacuate this hurt through irony, replying to Del's question, "What are you going to spend it on?" by saying, "I could always send away for a box of Bibles" (101). Freud comments on the use of jokes and irony in lifting repression, but adds, "as a rule, the repression is only temporarily lifted and is promptly reinstated" ("Repression" 150).

The text enacts both this lifting of repression and its reinstatement in a densely poetic moment. The scene takes place in the kitchen, where Del and her mother are cooking, talking, and working at a crossword puzzle. Sounds of Fern, the boarder, and of Owen, Del's brother, entering the house have been mentioned. Then, following her mother's ironic retort, Del comments: "Just before Fern came in one door and Owen came in the other, there was something in the room like the downflash of a wing or knife, a sense of hurt so strong, but quick and isolated, vanishing" (101).

In the instant at which irony allows a temporary release from the constant effort of repression, there is something like a "downflash," a word that suggests movement, light, and speed, almost an effect of lightning. This simile is then qualified through the paradoxical phrasing "of a wing or knife." Associated with "downflash," these signifiers offer both the image of a bird in movement – taking off or landing – and the metallic movement of a knife being stabbed downwards. The associations opened up here are those of flight from pain and, at the same time, of hurt and cutting, so that the image condenses the possibilities of escape and of reactivated pain. Taking into account that, elsewhere in the story cycle, images of birds in flight signify distress for Del's mother, such as "Alarm in my mother's voice was like the flap of rising wings" ("Lives of Girls and Women" 167), it would seem that the positive connotation of "wing" is overwhelmed by associations with distress and pain, and of being cut to the quick: the intrusion into consciousness of the mother's hurt is painful – "a sense of hurt so strong" – and the lifting of repression is therefore "quick and isolated, vanishing."[12]

Framing this pain, the almost stage-like setting offers compensatory elements to provide figurative consolation for the mother; she is in the kitchen in the company of her daughter, with doors about to open on either side, like arms, or again, wings, opening to embrace her, as her friend and her son enter. Here, Del's mother is not merely the victim of her desolate past; she is also the affective centre of her present. As the story closes, Del's mother is looking for the name of an Egyptian god with four letters to fill in a crossword puzzle: when Del suggests "Isis," putting a goddess in place of the missing god, it may be seen as a form of gift to her mother, reinstating her as the all-powerful mother, "the priestess" of her early childhood when Del had supposed her "powerful, a ruler" (89). The mother unconsciously recognizes this gift in an emotionally paradoxical formulation: "Isis is a goddess, I'm surprised at *you*" (101). Del's mother reaffirms her mastery in the domain of knowledge by correcting her daughter's error, and if this reaffirmation may also be seen as an expression of disappointment – "surprised at *you*" – it is also, through the italicization of *you*, the mark of the mother's implicit confidence in her daughter's intellectual potential.

Del's position as witness to her mother's moment of hurt, her role in the narrating of this moment, and the subsequent scene of sharing between them temporarily place the budding mother-daughter conflicts under truce. It is a moment of compromise in which the daughter tries to see her mother, not only as her mother, but as a woman with a personal, sometimes painful, history of her own. Having explored the emotional heritage of her maternal line, Del will begin exploring her own paths and negotiating her own libidinal investments. The story cycle does not align the daughter with the turning away from sexual pleasure that characterizes both mother and grandmother, but rather, develops constantly renegotiated positions between sexual exploration and artistic sublimation for its central figure, Del.

"Princess Ida" is only one, and not the first, in a long series of attempts by Munro to negotiate her relationship with the mother figure. This mother had already appeared in the stories of *Dance of the Happy Shades*, and she will reappear regularly in the author's work in "scenes that pop up anytime, like lantern slides, against the cluttered fabric of the present" ("Princess Ida" 83): sometimes, as we saw in the previous chapter, in disguise, as a semi-wicked (step)mother complicit in a beating ("Royal Beatings," *Who Do You Think You Are,* and again in "Fathers," *The View*), sometimes in dreams of forgiveness ("Friend of My Youth," *Friend*), occasionally as a sideline moral commentator ("The Wilds of Morris Township," *View*), or as a triumphant saleswoman, a "lady … whose offerings added a unique distinction" ("Working for a Living" 152–3, *View*). Nevertheless, "Princess Ida" stands as the first to give the mother her due, to see her as complex woman with a past and emotional density of her own; within this story, she is seen not *only* as a source of pain, embarrassment, and guilt for the daughter, but also as a woman of will, courage, tenacity, and resilience.

"Boys and Girls"

The Assumption of Sexed Subjectivity

"Boys and Girls" is an aptly named story that raises the question of sexual identity; how does a child come to assume a sexed position as a boy or a girl? A retrospective first-person narrative, this story from Munro's earliest collection (*Dance of the Happy Shades*, 1968) focuses on the thoughts and feelings of a young girl living in 1940s rural Ontario (Canada) in the period leading up to her adolescence. While the girl struggles with the increasingly conflictual tension between her sense of self and the place determined for her as a female child within her family and social framework, the narrative unexpectedly offers a response from the real, the enigma of subjectivity figured as a space-time wherein language fails and the body, in its symptomatic jouissance, speaks; a place beyond oedipal identifications and from which the truth of a sexed position of being emerges, imposing upon the subject the question of its recognition, acknowledgement, and assumption.

To this determining moment in the subject's libidinal destiny, Munro gives the form of an "act": a defining decision that arises from the unconscious and engages the body such that *doing* and *being* are, for a fleeting moment, in absolute accord. Assumed by the subject, the act takes on the status of a founding personal truth.[1] In this sense, the story's deceptively simple title introduces a dynamic perspective, one that exceeds the explanatory categories of (biological) sex and (social-constructivist) gender in its approach to the most fundamental and persistent enigma of our being: that of sexual difference. My analysis aims to make visible, through a close reading of the story, Munro's intuitive grasp of the complexity of what Lacan names "sexuation," a process that confronts the subject, as a speaking being, with the necessity of assuming a sexed position within the logical universe of "a man" or "a woman."[2] Both positions have their moment in this story, but it is the dilemma of the girl to which "Boys and Girls" gives its attention most fully.

"A WORLD MY FATHER MADE"

Opening on the gently alliterative "My father was a fox farmer" (111), the story is situated within the orderly influence of the paternal sphere. In the early part of the story, which follows a recognizable oedipal trajectory, the girl's primary pleasure is to help her father outdoors in his work of raising foxes for their fur. What is inscribed in the preference for the outdoors is not so much the work as the presence of the father: it is work done "in my father's service" (117). The first scene situates the girl in the company of her brother, observing her father's pelting activities, watching as he skins the foxes, "delicately … removing the little clotted webs of blood and the bubbles of fat" (112). Here, the relation between the father and death – indeed, the father's control over life and death – is not frightening, but fascinating; it calls upon her desire to *see*.[3] Another sense, that which above all others evokes memory, is also mentioned: "Then there was the smell" (111). The pronouncement is charged with understated irony as the odour is despised by the mother. For the girl, however, it carries positive associations: "I found it reassuringly seasonal, like the smell of oranges and pine needles" (112). Through the girl's proximity to her father, death and its revelation of the meagre corporeality of the body – "the fox … looked surprisingly small, mean and rat-like, deprived of its arrogant weight of fur" (111) – is made tolerable, is perhaps even associated with desire. The foxes, over which the father has dominion, are part of the mystery of life and death, and they work metaphorically, as does the space of the "cellar" where the pelting takes place, to suggest the subterranean forces of human existence. With their "strong primitive odour" (112) and "their eyes burning, clear gold, in their pointed, malevolent faces … drawn exquisitely sharp in pure hostility" (115), the foxes may be seen to represent the untameable jouissance, the amoral libidinal force of the drive, against which the father, the paternal metaphor, stands as barrier: "Nobody but my father ever went into the pens." Moreover, he braves this danger at the risk of his own life: "he had twice had blood-poisoning from bites" (115).

This is the world that intrigues, fascinates, and attracts the child in the ages between eight and eleven in her late-oedipal period of identification with the father as site of the ego Ideal,[4] an identification not with his desiring position as a man but with "the words, norms and directives of [a] given cultural collective" (Sharpe). In the Lacanian reworking of the oedipal structure as developed by Freud, both boys and girls turn from their primary attachment to the mother (who, through her desire for her partner signals that she is not complete, that she is lacking something to which her partner's love may give an answer) to a secondary attachment to the father, now seen to be the embodiment of that "agency whose gaze I try to impress with my ego image, … the ideal I try to follow and actualize" (Žižek, *How to Read* 80).

In "Boys and Girls," the father is clearly a (minor, somewhat ironically constructed) godlike figure in the child's eyes: "Alive, the foxes inhabited a world my father made for them" (114). Here, the word "alive" lifts the banality of the statement off the ground and infuses the image with life, associating the existence of the foxes with the creational act of the father, even as it introduces the possibility or the threat that the foxes could, under other, unnamed conditions, cease to be alive. Permitted into this world, the girl describes all the jobs accomplished in the service of her father's work (carrying water, raking the cut grass) and affirms that she "worked willingly under his eyes, and with a feeling of pride" (115–16). She thereby expresses her identification with and enjoyment of this Ideal Other, who is clearly situated in the field of the masculine, as her bedtime fantasies suggest: "[The fantasies] took place in a world that was recognizably mine, yet one that presented opportunities for courage, boldness and self-sacrifice, as mine never did. I rescued people from a bombed building … I shot two rabid wolves who were menacing the schoolyard … I rode a fine horse spiritedly down the main street of Jubilee, acknowledging the townspeople's gratitude for some yet-to-be-worked-out piece of heroism" (113–14). These fantasies offer prospects of imaginary (ego-satisfying) recognition from the social sphere that the father symbolizes within the rural world they inhabit. The girl mentions none of the activities associated with her mother, suggesting that she has detached herself from her primary love object and its attendant identifications; in other words, she has recognized that the mother does not have the phallus.

"NOT TO BE TRUSTED"

What place can the mother occupy in this context? Within the story, she is mainly an unwanted presence, marginalized by the girl who emphasizes their differences. In contrast with her own feelings, the mother "disliked the whole pelting operation" (115); she is judged "out of place" in the father's domain: "It was an odd thing to see my mother down at the barn" (116); and she is unwelcome in the girl's eyes: "I felt my mother had no business down here and I wanted [my father] to feel the same way" (117). The mother constitutes a rival for the girl's place in her father's attention and, further, a menace for her freedom of movement, bearing as she does the transmission of the social constraints of sexual roles: "She was plotting now to get me to stay in the house more, although she knew I hated it (because she knew I hated it) and keep me from working for my father. It seemed to me she would do this simply out of perversity, and to try her power" (118). The mother is therefore "not to be trusted," an "enemy" (117) from the perspective of the child who senses the threat of being evicted from her place in her father's attentions, all the more so as her younger brother, Laird (meaning Lord, landlord), is lurking in the background, being pushed forward by the mother as heir to the father's sphere. This threat of loss is what the girl has been studiously trying to keep at bay, hoping, one might say, that her place in her father's gaze might remain intact in its present form, in the relative lack of differentiation of childhood social-sexual roles.

Moreover, these roles are in the process of being complicated by the girl's awakening to the world of sexual desire. At one moment, the narrator's resentment toward her mother subsides long enough to acknowledge her role in authorizing the girl's sexual sense of self:[5] "If she was feeling cheerful, [she] would tell me all sorts of things – the name of a dog she had had when she was a little girl, the names of boys she had gone out with later on when she was grown up, and what certain dresses of hers had looked like – she could not imagine now what had become of them" (115). A quick look at this list of anecdotes shows that they concern the displacement of the mother's affections: from attachment to a pet, to a list of boys she dated, to her sense of herself as feminine in her recollection of her own appearance, for which the dresses are the metonym. In sharing with her daughter this sense of herself as a desiring and desirable woman, she is implicitly including her daughter in the sphere of desirable women, or quite simply, speaking to her "as a woman." If we accept the proposition that "in order to desire, one must first see oneself as desirable" (Fiumanò), the importance of this gift of the mother, for whom feminine desire is not nothing, can be recognized.

In contrast with the mother's talkative moments, the father is a quiet man: "My father did not talk to me unless it was about the work we were doing" (115). It is therefore unexpected when he offers her oblique praise in front of the "feed salesman," saying: "Like to have you meet my new hired man." In response, the girl "turn[s] away and rake[s] furiously, red in the face with pleasure" (116). This blush of embarrassment and pleasure is her bodily response to the public recognition that she is *seen*, and a great part of her pleasure consists in that fact of being seen; the father's gaze is the site from which she accedes to awareness that she is not transparent, she is an object of perception for the Other. Lacan associates this "being seen" with the feminine position: "this all-seeing aspect is to be found in the satisfaction of a woman who knows that she is being looked at, on condition that one does not show her that one knows that she knows" (Lacan, *SXI* 74–5). It is the presence of the third party – the feed salesman, a double figure for the father, but notably one who stands outside the family and who therefore is not subject to the incest taboo[6] – that reveals the unspoken knowledge in circulation, the truth of the girl's jouissance, that appears in a blush.[7] The salesman hits the nail on the head when he remarks, "Could of fooled me ... I thought it was only a girl" (116), exposing the fact that, in spite of the father's kidding remark that negates the sex of his daughter by conferring on her the status of "hired man," the question of sexual positioning is indeed at stake. Moreover, the feed salesman proleptically employs the very words – "only a girl" – with which the father will later ratify his daughter's sexuation. Because this doubled gaze of the father is valued by the girl, who responds to it "with pleasure," it fulfils the condition necessary to become the *cause* of her own desire: "It is the desire-causing look that determines for [a woman] what Freud called 'object choice'" (Fink 91–2).

"NO SUCH THING"

How far does this object-choice, which follows the classic oedipal pattern, go toward determining the girl's sexual identity? According to Colette Soler, it is not decisive: "sexed identity is not effected through object-choice" (*What Lacan Said* 180). This view is corroborated by Pickmann, who affirms:

> In the operation of substitution [from mother to father as object-choice], a girl does not discover the production of the new signified that she expects, the one that will tell her what Woman is. Worse than that, the apparent universality of the phallic signifier can only reflect back to her the radical absence of a feminine trait of identification.
>
> The eruption of sexual difference into the ideal, phallic world of childhood, leaves the subject who "knows" that she is a girl lacking an identity, and this, at the same moment that she is confronted by the lack in the (m)Other. It is as if the advent of sexual difference in the world deprives the girl of an existence thus far founded on sexual identity [i.e., identity with the mother] and on the guarantee of the existence of an Other ideal, phallic and worthy of love. (171)

In this perspective, not only is the object-choice *not* the defining element in sexual identity, but the resolution of the Oedipus conflict also leaves the girl bereft of what sense of identity she previously possessed; from an initial position of identification with the mother, seen as all-powerful, she can only identify with a mother now seen as lacking, and lacking in particular in any defining trait that situates her positively as "Woman." The girl is not provided with any self-evident indication of what, as a woman, she is to be.

The mother's role in "Boys and Girls" is essentially to relay or mediate the norms and codes of society, and gendered social roles in particular. Doubled briefly through the figure of the grandmother who is evoked and then dismissed – "My grandmother came to stay with us for a few weeks" (119) – the reinforced maternal line sets about defining the space and codes of "girls" who "don't slam doors," who "keep their knees together," and who help their mothers in the kitchen and don't ask questions (119). The child's reaction is to dismiss or resist these injunctions, since they suggest nothing other than restriction – "I continued to slam the doors and sit as awkwardly as possible, thinking that by such measures, I kept myself free" (119). Nevertheless, she becomes progressively more aware that for others, defining a girl was largely a question of behavioural codes and of social value: "The word *girl* had formerly seemed to me innocent and unburdened, like the word *child*, now it appeared that it was no such thing. A girl was not, as I had supposed, simply what I was, it was what I had to become. It was a definition, always touched with emphasis, with reproach and disappointment" (119).[8] However, if adherence to particular forms of behaviour is what defines a girl's social existence, then the girl in question would clearly prefer not to *be* that.

"THE LAW OF SEXUAL DIFFERENCE"

At this point, midway way through "Boys and Girls," the questions of the gendering forces of the family (based in the final instance on anatomical differences between the sexes) and of romantic object-choice or identifications have been brought to the fore, yet the question of feminine identity has not been resolved for the girl. If she has arrived at a provisional sense that *a girl* was something one "had to become," that still begs the question: how does one become a girl? The Lacanian answer: "by choice" (*SXX* 71).

To engage with this proposition, we need to shift our focus away from anatomical and cultural definitions: that is not where the choice is situated. It is a choice, rather, of *assuming the symbolic castration* that makes of us sexed beings and situates us within the logical universe that supports a man's or a woman's subjectivity. Lacan's table of sexuation (*SXX* 78) shows the logical universe of Man on the left side and of woman on the right:

$$\exists x\ \overline{\Phi x} \qquad\qquad \overline{\exists x}\ \overline{\Phi x}$$

$$\forall x\ \Phi x \qquad\qquad \overline{\forall x}\ \Phi x$$

Following Joan Copjec's gloss on the tables (*Read My Desire* 214), the formulas read as follows:

There is at least one x that is not submitted to the phallic function	There is not one x that is not submitted to the phallic function
All x's are (every x is) submitted to the phallic function	Not all (not every) x is submitted to the phallic function

The phallic function is *not* the function of access to omnipotent power, but rather its renunciation. It is synonymous with the function of castration that *limits* the ways in which jouissance may be obtained. This phallic function (Φx) appears on both sides of the table, but not in the same manner; the masculine and the feminine sides are two different stances in relation to this function, which, following Copjec, "is the law of sexual difference … a law of unconscious necessity, which is to say, it is a law that founds culture and is not a cultural law" (*Imagine* 222). To visualize this difference, I have borrowed and combined diagrams based on set theory from Fink (*The Lacanian Subject* 109, 112) and Morel (89). We note first of all that the logic of the masculine side forms a *closed set* since it is constituted by a limit based on a grounding exception.

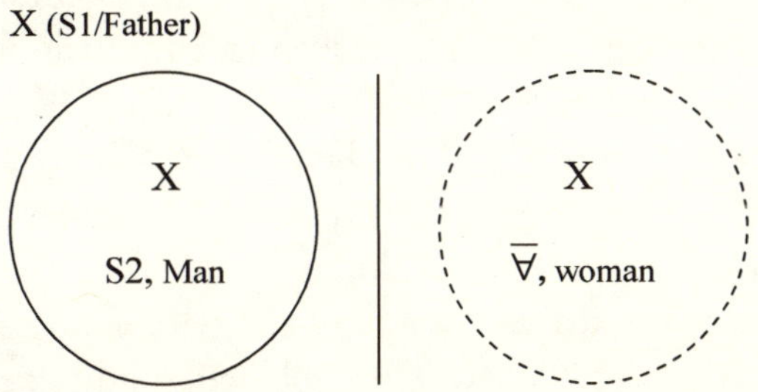

In other words, there is *at least one* that stands outside the rule (the mythical father of the primal horde) by virtue of which all others are submitted to it. The feminine side recognizes no grounding exception – "there is not one x" – and *the set cannot be closed*: those subjects situated there receive no defining signifier, there is no "exceptional One" to emulate. For a woman, the set (to which she belongs, without exception) is experienced as something of an open question lacking in consistency.[9]

Lacan affirms: "In adulthood, it is the destiny of speaking beings to divide themselves up into men and women" (*SXVIII*, 20 January 1971), from which it follows that "Every speaking being situates itself on one side or the other" of the table (*SXX* 79). We are therefore placed before a forced choice, a paradoxical one that, as Colette Soler points out, "in common experience, would attest, instead, to the rigors of constraint; subjects either recognize themselves so fully in their sexed aspirations that they suppose that the latter come from nature, or on the contrary, they feel so much that these positions have been forced on them that they live them out only as a symptom and in a state of pain … In reality, *the one who is designated as the subject, far from being the agent of this choice, bears its brunt*" (178–9, my emphasis). Nevertheless, it is equally important to keep in view that "in authorizing themselves as sexed beings … subjects are constrained by the fault of the speaking unconscious" (Soler 179) to assume this unasked for but inescapable choice between the phallic All and the Not-All phallic.

It is this notion of the *assumption of a sexed position* that I shall explore through my reading of the second half of "Boys and Girls."[10]

"A NEW WARINESS"

The question of sexed identity is written onto the mental landscape of the preadolescent girl through displacement onto the figures of two horses: Mack and Flora, M & F, Male and Female. Significantly, the horses enter the story by way of the sudden filling in of a gap in memory: "I have forgotten to say what the foxes were fed" (118). In the animal imagery of the story, the foxes, we have seen, function as representatives of the drives; moreover, these fox-drives belong to the father, and they need to be fed. They will be fed horse meat. Both the male and female horses are destined to undergo the *same* radical fate – death; their deaths offer the children, who are witnesses to these scenes, alternative modes of facing their own symbolic castration: Mack's way or Flora's.

The first killing scene concerns Mack, the male horse. Here, a second instance of forgetting characterizes the girl's perception of events: "'Are you going to shoot him today?' I said. Mack and Flora had been in the stable so long I had almost forgotten they were going to be shot" (120). In order to "see," "and know" what this killing / castration is, she disobeys her father's instructions to "Go on up and play around the house" and instead, takes her brother Laird, goes into the barn, sits on a beam in the loft, and peers through a knothole (121). The scene is thus framed and distanced by the wall that both divides the children from the killing field *and* gives them access to it in a restricted, focused way. They see two things: Mack's docility in the acceptance of his death, and the father's unflinching resolve in causing it: "My father raised the gun and Mack looked up as if he had noticed something and my father shot him" (122). Laird is the one who reacts to the scene. He registers surprise in his throat and body, emitting "a long, groaning breath of surprise when the shot was fired" and then, seeing the agonizing horse's legs flail for a moment, he clutches at the possibility that the horse has survived this death blow: "He's not dead," he says, as if there might be a way to submit to symbolic castration and yet remain free of its consequences. A moment later, as the horse's "muscles quivered and sank" (123), death is confirmed. Laird registers this moment of confrontation with the law of the father: "His expression was not frightened or upset, but remote, concentrating" (123). Flora's turn comes "two weeks later," and it is the girl who is subjectively interpellated by the female horse's death. This occurs in three different stages: a before, an atemporal present moment, and an after.

Before

Prior to the scene itself, the young heroine expresses the feeling that ever since the killing of Mack, something has changed for her: "I felt a little ashamed, and there was a new wariness, a sense of holding-off in my attitude to my father and his work" (124). It is *not* the *fact* of killing that has altered her feeling as she states: "I did not have any great feeling of horror or opposition, such as a city child might have had; I was too used to seeing the death of animals as a necessity by which we lived" (123–4). So what accounts for this change in her view of her father? In the paragraph that immediately precedes this statement of wariness, the girl gives expression to several things: her intention *not* to watch the killing of Flora, the experience of looking at herself in a mirror, and the memory of her father shooting Mack: "This time I didn't think of watching it. That was something to see just one time. I had not thought about it very often since, but sometimes, when I was busy, working at school, or standing in front of the mirror combing my hair and wondering if I would be pretty when I grew up, the whole scene would flash into my mind; I would see the easy, practiced way my father raised the gun, and hear Henry laughing when Mack kicked his legs in the air" (123). In this structural repetition of the "mirror phase" moment, the imaginary unity of the child's self-image is disrupted, first by internal anxiety as the girl questions the adequation between her own image and the ideals of femininity that she presupposes, and second by the intrusion of the symbolic father who appears in a "flash" as the gaze, the location of the ego-Ideal, in this mirror-image scene.

But this paternal gaze is suddenly complicated: the father is in his role as the exception who guarantees, by *embodying* it, the limit of the symbolic law; he is the faithful upholder of its neutral necessity. Yet he is accompanied (and therefore the girl is also gazed at) by Henry, the hired hand, who functions as the underside of that benevolent neutrality, as the real father of unrestrained jouissance. Throughout the story, Henry has appeared as a figure of lewd pleasure – bodily and bawdily oriented, he coughs, laughs, keeps calendars of pin-up girls[11] in his nook of the barn, and gets a kick out of death: first in the opening scene of the story, when he "takes a swipe" at the girl with a sack full of the "naked slippery bodies" of pelted foxes, exclaiming "Christmas present!" (112). Then in the above mirror scene, which replays what the children saw, he's heard "laughing" at the dying horse. From the conjoined presence of the two men came, and comes again, the shot that kills the horse: this mark of symbolic castration, which includes the knowledge of mortality, draws a line, materialized in sound, sight, and effect, before the onlooking children. The guardedness the girl feels toward her father is not a manifestation of moral reproach, but *the unconscious recognition of sexual difference* as such. Hence, she feels "a little ashamed" (124), exposed in her knowledge of sexual difference, and perhaps ashamed also at what she knows about the masculine fiction supported by the law of castration: the law is upheld, but it is *not* neutral, it also enjoys itself.[12] The "wariness" she feels is an index of this newly acquired knowledge.

During

The proposition I have put forward is that the two horses symbolize the masculine and feminine sexed positions, each of which involves a particular stance in relation to the law of the symbolic order. Unlike the obedient male horse, Mack, who submits to the law by accepting to be led by the halter to his death, Flora fights to escape her fate: "She had broken away from [Henry]. She was running free in the barnyard, from one end to the other. It was exciting to see her running, whinnying, going up on her hind legs, prancing and threatening like a horse in a Western movie" (124). The girl is enjoying her position as chance spectator to this exciting scene when, suddenly, she is called upon to become a participant: her father gives the command "Go shut the gate!" (124). Her initial impulse, full of imaginary at-oneness of body and purpose, is to comply with her father's order. So she runs toward the gate to close it: "I could run very fast. I ran across the garden, past the tree where our swing was hung, and jumped across a ditch into the lane. There was the open gate. She had not got out, I could not see her up on the road; she must have run to the other end of the field. The gate was heavy. I lifted it out of the gravel and carried it across the roadway. I had it half way across when she came in sight, galloping straight towards me" (124–5). At this moment, where jumping across a ditch prefigures the metaphorical transition of the child to the position of sexed being, she gives her response to her father's command: "Instead of shutting the gate, I opened it as wide as I could" (125). It is a statement proffered without excuses or justifications; it presents the accomplishment of the action as something entirely unmotivated, to be understood in its own self-evidence, as if this gesture of opening came from a place she had no awareness of, borne, as it were, of its own necessity. In that sense, the opening of the gate has the structure, not of an action, but of *an act*, understood in the following way:

> [Any] act worthy of the name isn't deduced; it isn't a deliberation; [it is] neither a calculation nor a compromise. Even if a careful consideration of the pros and cons precedes it, one recognizes an act as that which exceeds its reasons. That's why the act is foundational, primordial, creative. Every act worthy of the name creates a new truth, which isn't by virtue of that fact eternal, but which has a chance to be unforgettable for the subject supported by this act. Thus the act creates a truth eternized in the subject, who changes because of it … To be in the act, it is necessary not to think. (Miller, "Σ(x)")

Indeed, the text confirms that the girl's gesture is not thought out in advance: "I did not make any decision to do this, it was just what I did"; it is not motivated and comes as a surprise to the girl herself – "I could not understand why I had done it." Moreover, the very quantity of self-reflexive commentary on the action signals the unprecedented nature of it. It is an event that imposes the subjective necessity of itself both during and after the fact: "I did not regret it; when she came running at me and I held the gate open, that was the only thing I could do" (125). Holding the gate open, she *is* the open set of the feminine side; she stands there as the locus of the failure of the symbolic order, of the father's law, and of language to encompass her being.

Munro lifts this act out of the flow of time by framing it. Placed between the agitation of her own attempts to shut the gate, and her brother's "scrambling out of the ditch" to help her, the moment is suspended in time: preceded by "just time to get the chain on" and followed by a thrice repeated "too late," it is held in-between, untouched by markers of temporality. Outside of cause and consequence, in intuitive response to Flora "galloping straight towards [her]," and mirroring Flora's refusal to comply, the girl makes a choice: "instead" of one thing, she does another. Time then reasserts itself around this moment of exception, this pulsation of the unconscious, itself outside of time and logic.

After

In narrative terms, the effect of this irruption of the real must find its symbolic inscription: to this founding, creative act, the girl retroactively attributes meaning, signifying her new subjective truth by declaring herself to be "on Flora's side" (125). The use of the word "side" clearly has its oppositional force in the context of Flora fleeing the father's gun, but the girl knows that she only postpones Flora's fate in opening the gate. Death will come. Hence, the side she is on is less to do with active, goal-oriented transgression than with an unconscious positioning related to being: in that sense, it is an act that she "undergoes" rather than "accomplish[es]" (Žižek, *Enjoy* 51) even if the result has a transgressive aspect to it.[13] Transgression implies both the recognition of a limit and a refusal to respect it; the father's call to shut the gate is the call of the One to recognize (in the sense of "to treat as valid") the limits or the law of the masculine set. The girl's nonvalidation of the limit locates her being on the *side* of those subjects who, while being produced within the symbolic order, maintain an internal distance to the law of the signifier: this internal distance is represented by the splitting of the figure of the girl, where Flora (the girl-as-unconscious drive) runs beyond the gate,[14] while the girl (as daughter) does not step outside the enclosed area.[15] In this contradictory way, she experiences, and immediately assumes, her mode of symbolic castration: the feminine mode. That she makes this "obscure decision of [her] being" (Soler, *Lacan* ch. 13) and unconsciously *knows* (even if the content of the knowledge remains enigmatic) that this choice will henceforth determine her place in the symbolic order are correlated to the fact that her father, as its representative, must *recognize* the significance of her act if she is not to be cast out of the community. She anticipates, with a certain tone of loss, that he will do so: "And when my father found out about it, he would know that I was not entirely on his side" (125). In other words, through her act she has assumed her sexed position as a woman, as a being within the phallic-symbolic order, but not entirely.

RATIFYING THE CHOICE

The return of the men after the capture and killing of Flora allows for the textual representation of the newly affirmed position of each child. First of all, there is Laird, who, even earlier, on seeing the gate wide open, echoed his father's command "yelling, 'Shut it, shut it!' even after it was too late" (125) and who, seeing the men setting off after the runaway horse called out "Let me go too, let me go too!" (125).[16] Finally, upon returning from the expedition, "Laird lifted his arm to show off a streak of blood. 'We shot old Flora,' he said, 'and cut her up in fifty pieces'" (127). Thus, with great economy of style, Munro puts forth Laird's newly acquired place among men, identified as the agent of castration in killing Flora through the insignia of the blood on his arm, which picks up on the earlier image of the father seen "[coming] from the meathouse; [with] his stiff bloody apron on" (116); furthermore, he is identified with the excess of the law as he unselfconsciously enjoys and exhibits his new power, raising his phallic arm covered in female blood. This bloody image also links sexuation to the inescapability of death and sexual reproduction, or in other words, to our mortality. Endowed with visible signs of his new symbolic status, Laird becomes a zealous supporter of the limits of the law. Eager to show which side he is on, he denounces his sister: "Anyway it was her fault Flora got away" (127).

In contrast with her brother, there is nothing visible for the girl to display, no sign of "being a girl" that can find its inscription in the symbolic environment. Everything then hangs on the father's reaction, as locus of the ego-Ideal. His first reaction is "disgust" and accusatory questioning: "What did you do that for?" (127). But the girl has no words to communicate her experience, grounded as it is in the failure of the signifier. Her silence is extended to the entire group – "For some time nobody said anything" (127) – marking the collective intuition that something unnamed is awaiting its signifier, or in other words, that the lack in the Other is under threat of being exposed. The mother is silent. It is the father who then gives the event its communal meaning or symbolic inscription, paradoxically ratifying the girl's choice: "'Never mind,' my father said. He spoke with resignation, even good humour, the words that absolved and dismissed me for good. 'She's only a girl,' he said" (127). Defined as a girl, she is "absolved" from guilt – and therefore not sent away from the communal table – because she is not called upon to incarnate the limit in the same way that Laird is; by the same token, she is "dismissed," or in other words, excluded from the sphere of the phallic "all," the closed set of the universal masculine.

Understandably, most critical commentary on this passage highlights the deflation of the girl by focusing on the adverb "only": according to Nischik, the girl "seems to have lost the gender battle" (216). In this reading, the father voices the social discourse that relegates the feminine to a place of inferiority or perhaps even of insignificance. This question cannot be eluded. "A sixteen-year-old female reader" of "Boys and Girls" wrote this letter to Munro: "I keep hoping the girl will win out; the ending is a cutting, crushing blow for me. I do not want to be a girl. I still believe that is the rottenest thing that can happen to someone. I inwardly protest it. It is a conflict I am not able to resolve; perhaps you have an answer" (qtd in McCaig 157). The despondent complaint of this reader speaks of a frustration at this absence of any stable point of identification in the feminine position, whereby a woman may feel stranded, adrift, or devalorized in her self-perception.[17]

And yet, this is not where the force of the story lies. The lack in *having* of the feminine side need not obscure the positive assumption of a sexed position which, by virtue of its being not wholly subjected to the phallic function, opens onto the possibility of a surplus in being, a being "in the gap." Unlike the sixteen-year-old reader, the protagonist does not "inwardly protest": on the contrary, she affirms: "I didn't protest that, even in my heart. Maybe it was true" (127). This final line in the story is the point at which the semblance of meaning stops and ambivalence floods the discursive space: *what* doesn't she protest? What is the "it" that may be "true"? "Girl"? Or "only"? What does "only" mean? What does "girl" mean? And then, what can "only a girl" possibly mean, in particular to a girl? Small wonder the sixteen-year-old reader cannot resolve the question. And yet, the hopelessness of giving any positive content to "only a girl" negates neither the force of the girl's choice not to protest the father's pronouncement, nor her recognition of a potential truth value – "Maybe it was true" – in it, where something is given and something is taken away; where the attribution of a lack is paradoxically a gift. In naming her a "girl," the father symbolically recognizes her sexual position, such that she considers it settled "for good"; she is thereby reassured that from the vantage point of the desire of the Other, she is recognized as a "girl."

This recognition corresponds to the unconscious truth of her subjectivity at the level of both desire and drive. First, there has been a shift from the fantasy position of phallic dominance (her earlier "rescuer on horseback" fantasies) to that of desired object: it is after the gate episode, but before the return of the men, in an interlude of expectancy, that the narrating voice inserts the information that "lately" the girl's bedtime fantasies had undergone "mysterious alterations"; no longer the rescuer, she has moved into a new position: "somebody would be rescuing me. It might be a boy from our class at school, or even Mr. Campbell, our teacher, who tickled girls under the arms."[18] She has gone from occupying the position of *having* the phallus (social status and recognition) in earlier fantasies, to *appearing* as the object of masculine desire; indeed the fantasies no longer have an end point of ego valorization, but get sidetracked by considerations such as "what I looked like" or, picking up on her mother's earlier stories, "what kind of dress I had on" (126).[19] In this context, there is an unconscious truth for the girl that is related to the desire of the Other, and that finds itself in agreement with the feminine position as object of desire: where "masculine and feminine distinctions are determined not by 'psychic' essence or behaviour ... but [may be understood] as gender nonspecific identifications as lover (active) or beloved (passive)" (Ragland, *The Logic of Sexuation* 22), the girl situates herself, in the field of desire, as the feminine beloved.[20]

Second, the bodily animal incarnation of Flora gives literary representation to the real as living substance – the *en-corps* of jouissance – and "lays bare the drive-fixations" that are "decisions of the body" (Verhaeghe 63). Through her own bodily decision to open the gate, the girl echoes the female horse's physical refusal of the limit; metaphorically, the site of the drive transfers to her. The girl has given bodily expression to her subjectivity as fixed by the drive: here, beyond all reason and language, she is the *letter* or let-*her*, the one who does not close the gate. Finally, the nagging question that could not be settled through reflection, gender coding, or anatomical attributions finds a solution through her encounter with the constraint of symbolic castration and the necessity of its inscription either within the logic of the phallic closed set or in the not-all open set. The nomination by the father and her ensuing assumption of the word "girl" offers her respite from the deadlock of the noncorrespondence of the sexes. She does not protest it because it is the truth of her sexuation as witnessed by her act.

THE ONE AND ONLY

The importance of the father's recognition through naming should not be brushed aside or denigrated. According to Danielle Bergeron, "[The] Father's word of love, manifesting his love for his girl in the absence of sexual lust [is what] situates her as subject in the order of language and manages the libidinous writing of the body by uniting it under a distinct Ego. The limiting by the father of the Other's *jouissance* insisting in the girl-child's body inscribes the mark of lack and situates the girl in the register of the desiring subject" (13).[21] And yet, the diminutive "only" of the father's pronouncement would seem to stand in the way of any joyful assumption of this place, signalling all too clearly that the symbolic order is antagonistic to the not-all.[22] "Only a girl" exemplifies the very characteristic masculine need to defame women at the very moment that their otherness is acknowledged, an ironic recognition that her position as not-all is threatening, needs to be contained, lest it contaminate the All of Man who has paid the price to indicate that he is not a woman. Perhaps the girl's "Maybe it was true," both tentative and absolute, includes the acknowledgment of the paradox that being recognized as a girl, or as a boy, involves a loss, the loss of a previous state of not-knowing about sexual difference.[23] If Laird's jubilant ignorance of the loss involved on the masculine side seems to be a more comfortable position, it will nonetheless determine him in an orientation that requires his participation in the fiction of phallic consistency, against the truth that the symbolic order he will be called to support is, in spite of appearances, not-all.[24]

Could we not see this "only" pronounced by the father as the signifier of his own structural limitation, that of his place within the closed masculine set? Loyal to the myth of the One, he expulses the inassimilable feminine Other through this "only," but unbeknownst to him, in the logic of the open set, this "only" is the space of "the *poesis* – the something coming from nothing – that Lacan links to the contingency of being and, ultimately, to the path of love" (Barnard, "Tongues" 172): its productive lack of definition opens onto positive associations with the concept of "singularity." *Only* is defined, among other things, as "uniquely, specially, [or] pre-eminently" (OED). Indeed, it functions as something of a primal word whose meaning includes its opposite. Etymologically signifying "one-like," *only* has something of the One, but differs from it, remaining indefinite.[25] How could or why should the girl protest this "only," which refuses universalizing totality and thereby opens onto a myriad of inventive possibilities? Munro herself certainly doesn't protest it, but rather claims it as her own: "I feel that women have always had a clarity of vision which men were denied. And, in a way, this is a gift, it goes along with lack of power. And I valued that very much – the value of being able to see clearly" (qtd in Carrington 12–13). Here, Munro specifically associates feminine lack and clarity of vision; this vision is perhaps, quite simply, the knowledge that being, as such, cannot be encompassed by the phallic One and that the not-fully, not-wholly, not-all is not something less, but rather, something *else*. What can we know about this something else? *Nothing* in terms of a positive, definitive trait, but *something* perhaps if we conceive of it as a modality: the not-all is the mode that denies enclosure, or in other words, defends the truth of the open gate.

11

Feverish Feminine Transport: Desire, Jouissance, and Love

"Eskimo"

Fantasy and Beyond

Literary journeys of the intimate self are often represented through narratives of travel, and this is indeed the case in many of Munro's stories. By plane, train, truck, bus, car, or boat, on horseback or on a motorcycle, or then again, simply walking through the streets,[1] her characters are, often enough, on the move. The travelling is often fitful and agitated, corresponding to a moment of self-examination or self-discovery: the women in question (they are almost always women) are on inner voyages metaphorized out onto the space of the vehicle that contains or holds them, and the destination is rarely put forward as significant in itself. Something of their situation as desiring women is at stake: a love they are hoping for or being invited into, one that they are fleeing or being banished from. There is pleasure and pain in the process, there are intuitions and flashes of insight that erupt at the surface of consciousness, as if the trip suspended time, and the vibrations of the transport vessel gave voice and existence to the bodily self of desire and jouissance.

I have chosen to study two stories in this regard: "Eskimo" and "Too Much Happiness." The first takes place entirely on a plane, the second on a train, both with flashbacks to the contexts of the lives and loves of their protagonists. In both cases, the woman travelling is afflicted with a particular set of symptoms, namely, a sore throat and general feverishness: "Her throat feels slightly raw and her head heavy" ("Eskimo" 265); "And her sore throat and slight shivers, surely a full-fledged cold coming on her" ("Too Much Happiness" 268). I will argue that these bodily symptoms bear witness to conflicts between conscious and unconscious knowledge about desire. Both women feel out of place in the company of fellow travellers who are strangers to them and who reflect back to them some inner disharmony, some "strangerliness" within. The movement of the vehicles is not especially highlighted; the general effect is more to do with being momentarily taken out of the stream of social events and relationships and enclosed in a space where chronological time is suspended and unconscious time reframes experience. In this way, the voyage takes each woman toward some unexpected, unwished for, experience of the self.[2]

"ESKIMO"

It was on reading an article by Claude Maisonnat entitled "'Eskimo,' or An Encounter with the Real of Feminine Desire"[3] that I returned to "Eskimo" which, on first reading, appears to be a quirky, confusing story of disgruntled emotions. The main character, Mary Jo, is on a plane, headed for Tahiti. The trip is a present from her boss, the cardiologist, Dr Streeter, who is also her lover. A married man, he does not accompany her but sends her off to enjoy herself. During the flight, an encounter with an Eskimo girl who is accompanied by a dominating male partner sets off a series of troubling emotional reactions, fantasies, and dreams that intertwine with Mary Jo's feelings about Dr Streeter. At the heart of the story is the disturbing event of an onslaught of jouissance experienced by Mary Jo as overwhelming, unwanted "desire." The questions fan out from there: what is the significance of this experience for her? Why is it so disturbing and how does it relate to the logic of her subjective desire? What is the function of the Eskimo woman in this questioning of Mary Jo's subjectivity? How far can the work of interpretation take us in resolving the enigmas the story poses?

From the very start, the status of Mary Jo's flight to Tahiti is ambiguous: she is on a plane, going somewhere that she doesn't really want to go, going in spite of the fact that she doesn't want to go *anywhere*. The implicit explanation is that Mary Jo was given a present she couldn't find the resources within herself to refuse. Indeed, her boss has rewarded her, ostensibly for her dedicated work as his assistant, by offering her a trip to a tropical destination. The monetary value and social recognition that this implies make it symbolically difficult for her to refuse. Nevertheless, it is an unwanted gift, and worse, it recognizes the wrong thing: her work rather than her love. In accepting it, she betrays something important in herself – her desire. When we speak of desire, if we want to approach its truth value for the subject, we must turn to the fantasy that sustains it. "Eskimo" is a courageous attempt to approach the fantasy that sustains desire in a love relationship; in this case, it is a relationship that flies in the face of the dominant symbolic coordinates of our times, which attempt to frame desire and love relationships within the general movement toward "sexual equality." In this perspective, voiced by Streeter's daughter Rhea, a woman must refuse any position of nonequality with men, including within the sexual relationship. Mary Jo's relationship with Dr Streeter is shaped in a different way. My reading of the story will follow the imploding movement of the story of Mary Jo's love, desire, and jouissance.

LOVE

Love demands love. It never stops demanding it. It demands it … *encore.*

Lacan, *SXX* 4

What sustains Mary Jo's relationship to Dr Streeter is her love for him. She loves him, and desires to be loved by him in return. Her relationship to him is structured through her place as subordinate: he is the doctor, she is the nurse; he is married, she is his mistress. None of this seems to disagree with Mary Jo, any more than she is troubled by his racial bigotry and conservative certainties. She finds in her lover, cause for love: she loves in him that he is "the best cardiologist in that part of the country, because he gave himself over every day to the gray-faced people in his waiting room, the heart cases, people living in fear, in pain. His life was given over" (259). In this love, there is overdetermination: Streeter is not any sort of doctor, he is a specialist dealing in heart cases. Beyond the clear metaphor of her need to be loved, to have her "heart" cared for, we also note that Mary Jo's mother "had died of what was called 'heart disease' – something Mary Jo later knew was a heart problem that Dr Streeter could have detected and recommended surgery for" (261). His professional trappings, including his knowledge and authority, are, for Mary Jo, the sign of something greater within him, a form of dedication to his path of being: of being a man who is faithful to his doctor-destiny. It is in this sense that I understand Lacan's affirmation, quoted earlier, that "a woman can … love in a man only the way in which he faces the knowledge thanks to which he souloves" (*SXX* 88). This merging of "soul" and "love" points toward a certain conception of "the good" in which "each of the beings in the world can only orient itself toward the greatest being by confounding its good, its own good, with that with which the Supreme Being shines" (*SXX* 84–5).

The first element in Mary Jo's love, therefore, tends to associate Dr Streeter's fidelity to his "supreme cause" (his belief in the importance of his work as a doctor) with Mary Jo's mother, allowing for the retrospective fantasy that he might have "saved" her. The second element in this devotion is that Streeter is not a casual or an accidental saviour of the misery-stricken: on the contrary, "His life was given over." The passive structure here suggests that he does not see himself as the agent of his destiny, but that he was compelled on some level to serve this something greater than himself. It is in the courage with which Streeter meets his fate, his vocation, or his destiny, that Mary Jo finds cause for love. Her love therefore involves a form of admiration for his self-sacrificing adherence to a cause, one which situates him within the law and the social order: "An incurable, calm, and decent sadness is what he breathes out over the phone before you even hear his voice" (276). Decency, but also "obedience" is what Mary Jo focuses on, and at this point her understanding of Streeter, and of what she sees in him as characteristic of men, falters: "This sadness seems to come from obedience. Mary Jo can just recognize that, never understand it. She thinks there is an obedience about men that women can't understand. It's not the things he knows about – Mary Jo could manage that – but the things he accepts that make a difference. He baffles her, and compels her. She loves this man with a baffled, cautious, permanent love" (276). Obedience is the recognition and respect of a limit. What Mary Jo understands about Dr Streeter is that he is situated within the masculine logic of being whereby his very selfhood is constituted through the recognition of and obedience to a finite view of being, a being constituted by a limit. That Mary Jo can perceive but not understand this in him – she is "baffled" – situates *her* within the feminine structure.

This structure of being participates in Mary Jo's desire for Streeter. She loves in him the man whose life is given in obedience to the cause of saving the hearts of the ill. Next to that, all of the criticism that Streeter's daughter Rhea levels against her father has no purchase whatsoever on Mary Jo. Through Rhea, the story offers the voice of the social dictate, the symbolic superego, telling Mary Jo what she *should* feel, as opposed to what she does feel. Rhea embodies the commanding voice of a clichéd feminist discourse, whereby a man in power (as fathers, by structural necessity, are) is de facto an oppressive patriarch. As such, he is held responsible for the ills and evils of the goal-oriented, and therefore phallic, development of society. These evils include nuclear proliferation, acid rain, unemployment, racial bigotry, and the disadvantaged situation of women, and "her father is not far from being the cause of all this, in Rhea's mind" (257).

When Mary Jo brushes off Dr Streeter's discourse as "just his opinions" (257), Rhea confronts her, but in such a way that reveals Rhea herself to be behaving in the inconsiderate, dominating way she attributes to men, symbolically colonizing Mary Jo's space with her wet motorcycle helmet: "'Why, Mary Jo? Why do men have to have their opinions? So women can sit around clicking their tongues while men wreck the world?' She had taken off her motorcycle helmet and set it down, wet from the rain, on Mary Jo's desk. She was shaking out her long, dark, tangled hair. 'No man is wrecking my world,' said Mary Jo spiritedly, picking up the helmet and setting it on the floor" (258). Although Mary Jo's thoughts reveal that she "didn't feel as equal to this conversation as she sounded" (258), the reasons for her discomfort are related in part to her awkward position in relation to Rhea – as Rhea's father's mistress, she is a rival to Rhea's mother, and indirectly, to Rhea herself, but Mary Jo is also, on occasion, a substitute mother. In this context, Mary Jo knows that they are not really discussing feminism, politics, or environmental issues, but that Rhea is trying, through Mary Jo, to position herself in relation to her father: "She wanted and expected Mary Jo to defend her father, so that she could be amused and scornful … and at the same time, reassured" (258). In this sense, Maisonnat's reading of the story simply takes Rhea's discourse too literally when he affirms that "Rhea, Dr Streeter's daughter … is the one who speaks the truth about the shortcomings of her father, which Mary Jo blinds herself to or even attempts to justify" (73). This reading is based on the view that Streeter can be reduced to a single truth – that he is a bigoted, conservative man who lives a married life and has a mistress – which allows Maisonnat to affirm that Mary Jo, who is in no way blind to these facts, needs to make "the ethical choice" (81) and, following this logic, end her relationship with Streeter. In this way, criticism becomes the relay for the social script's superego injunction, telling the subject what the "correct" subjective choice would be.

As it happens, Mary Jo finds her own path to a critique of Streeter, but it is not on the basis of his politics. It is rather when he disturbs their usual pattern, a routine whereby "at the end of the day, Dr Streeter sometimes comes upstairs with her; she makes supper, and he stays for part of the evening" (265). But "love demands love. It never stops demanding it," says Lacan (*SXX* 4). Their ritual is, for Mary Jo, a sign of their love. It is only when Streeter departs from their semblance of domestic union that she is wounded and upset. By offering her a holiday abroad, on her own, he misinterprets her desire and responds instead to some superego injunction of his own along the lines of "Married men should repay their mistresses with a treat, such as a holiday." Rhea finds herself in agreement with her father's action, which tends to confirm that the gesture conforms with the implicit values of the period: "Not that he doesn't owe it to you. It's about time he paid you back some of your devotion, I think" (260). There is clearly an economic subtext here in the vocabulary of "owing" and being "paid back" for something; in this way, Mary Jo's love, given freely, is devalued, transformed into a product that must be paid for. In other words, she becomes Streeter's hooker.

In what sense does this reveal something to Mary Jo that she didn't already know? She knew, of course, that he was married, but by creating a negative portrait of his wife as a heavy drinker, "an unkempt, capricious, disruptive woman" (261), she could imagine Streeter's life with his wife as "prescribed, bleak and costly" (261); in other words, in Mary Jo's view of things, the wife was a burden, a responsibility, whereas *she* was chosen, she was the true *beloved*. In this perspective, being sent away to Tahiti is deeply wounding: it is a denial of Mary Jo's desire, which is *to be the chosen object of Streeter's desire*. Not for money, but for love.

It is a commonplace nowadays to associate a woman's willingness to be the object of a man's desire with the masochistic structure. Colette Soler writes an illuminating chapter in *What Lacan Said about Women* entitled "Are Women Masochistic?" wherein she distinguishes clearly between modalities of desire as witnessed in women and in perverse masochistic subjects, both of whom share the trait of being positioned as an object of the other's desire: "the masochist wants himself to be a disparaged object; he cultivates the appearance of something that has been cast off and makes himself into a piece of trash. A woman, on the contrary, dresses herself up in phallic brilliance in order to be the *agalmatic* [treasured] object" (76–7). Streeter, on the other hand, is situated within the masculine structure of desire, which finds in its desired object something that compensates for the phallic castration that is implied in his sexuation. What compensates for his lack is the surplus jouissance afforded by "possessing" the woman, who in her appearance as desirable, gives back the illusion, paradoxically, of phallic wholeness. To secure this desire of the man, the woman therefore works hard to mask her lack: in "Eskimo," Mary Jo focuses on her teeth as that part of herself that reveals her as lacking, and she anxiously tries to remedy her appearance on that score: "As soon as she had enough money, Mary Jo started getting some work done on her teeth. She was self-conscious about them; she never wore lipstick and was careful of how she smiled. She had her eyeteeth pulled and the front teeth filed. She still didn't like the way they looked, so she got braces" (262). This paragraph puts forward the structure of the feminine masquerade: in the interests of improving her desirability, Mary Jo both consolidates her lack – offering herself as "castrated" (removing and filing her teeth) – and covers it over with something shiny: her dental braces. Even if the braces are intended to come off, it so happens that Streeter first "liked her when her braces were still on. They were on the first time he made love to her" (262). The braces function as a metonym of the shiny "something more" that both signals and conceals the feminine position of lack. Given the locus of Mary Jo's fixation, it is not surprising that a great deal of the imagery in the short story will focus on the mouth, the teeth, the throat, on sucking and on licking.

To begin with, it is in her throat that Mary Jo experiences the uneasiness of her situation, precisely as dis-*ease*, through symptoms: "Something is wrong with her," "Her throat feels slightly raw and her head heavy" (265). What is a symptom? A symptom means "that we have a body that suffers. What does it suffer from? The body suffers from truth, precisely because it is inhabited by language, and truth complicates its relationship to the world and to the real. A body which can make itself ill from truth ceases to obey the knowledge within itself" (Canellopoulos). The story, I would suggest, supports the hypothesis that Mary Jo's symptom, her sore throat, is provoked by the consent she has given to the narcissistic wounding of her desiring self by having accepted the unwanted gift and got on the plane. She unconsciously knows this, since she reflects that "her body is protesting its removal too quickly … from its place of habitual attachment and rest" (265); this formulation focuses only on the symptomatic *effect* of bodily displacement, but leaves the *cause* of the symptom unacknowledged. The story and the encounter with the "Eskimo" girl will cipher this uneasy knowledge that Mary Jo has, but which, because she is unwilling to acknowledge it, she expresses somatically.

DESIRE

The arrival of the Eskimo woman in the flight cabin gives bodily focus to Mary Jo's unconscious self-questioning, but even before this stranger is introduced, the whole atmosphere in the plane attests to the disquiet of the protagonist. Everything and everyone annoys her: the Greek family with two children, the younger of which – a boy – "has a slight teething problem" (263) and whom the parents are at pains to feed, anxiously mopping up his drool; the Indian family with two little girls and a baby boy who "climbs on his mother's lap" to breastfeed and "settles there, lolls and sucks, with his eyes open, looking blissful and commanding" (264). To all this family concern with children and the feeding of the young, in particular the male child, Mary Jo is "surprised at how ill-disposed she feels" (263); "she is not used to feeling such aversion" (264). Maisonnat suggests that this aversion (which he reads as "jealousy") may be an index of what Mary Jo has given up in accepting her position as mistress to a married man, notably, maternity and the phallic child (77). This is possible, but more importantly, it seems that the focus on the feeding of the children and the markers of teething and sucking point to the oral component of the protagonist's disgruntled sexuality, to the opaque place of its fixation in the drive, or in other words, to the child Mary Jo once was, demanding something of the mother. The appearance of the Eskimo woman, with the mouth of a suckling babe, whose "front teeth are missing, all across the top," supports this reading: the woman will clearly function as a double for Mary Jo – not a narcissistic double, nor a social alter ego, but her double in the Lacanian real: an unsettling index of her sexual jouissance.

Like the Greek family from Australia, or the elegant Indian father listening to rock music, the Eskimo woman offers paradoxical signs: she seems ageless, with a "look of sly, durable merriment such as an old woman's smile might have, or a baby's" (267), she is accompanied by a man who could be, but is not, her father, whom Mary Jo imagines as the ruler of some vague Asian tribe seen on TV – the Khan (268). All of the age-indeterminate, ambiguously related, culturally confusing signs that Mary Jo is assailed by on the plane become concentrated in this figure of the Eskimo woman whose presence inaugurates the "veiled" phase in the story: the movie screen (of 1970s air travel) is lowered and the lights in the plane are dimmed (269).

Uninterested in the film, Mary Jo takes off her headphones and tunes in, symbolically, to the "other scene": the argument going on between the Eskimo woman and the "Khan" that has no clear object, but that reveals the structure of their relationship (and mirrors that of Mary Jo and Streeter's): he is a dominating man, sure of his authority over her, with potential to hurt – "He makes a feint to grab at her again, a swift, brutal movement, as if this time, next time, he intends really to hurt her" (270). The writing becomes dreamlike, where the words are comprehensible, but the meaning is obscure: the Eskimo girl sits in the empty seat beside Mary Jo repeating "Don't tell nobody. I am Eskimo." Maisonnat rightly notes that "the signifier 'Eskimo' comes to embody … the very notion of alterity as an irreducible difference," but in spite of his qualification that "the Eskimo girl must be seen as a figure of the double for Mary Jo, in so far as she embodies all the repressed, unwelcome aspects of her desire," Maisonnat retains this notion of alterity at the level of the imaginary-symbolic axis, noting that the "textual presentation of the [Eskimo] girl highlights her singularity" (78), in other words, attributes separate subjectivity to the girl. Is it not rather that the function of the character of the Eskimo girl is *entirely* indexed on Mary Jo's constructed subjectivity?

The alterity she designates is not that of the difference between two singular subjectivities (i.e., hers and another woman's) or between the conscious and the unconscious, but rather the irreducible gap between the unconscious fantasy (which the Eskimo girl embodies) and the drive to jouissance that gives life to it. The character of Eskimo points toward the real, which is veiled by fantasy and sustains, as drive, Mary Jo's desire. This is why, "at its most fundamental, the double embodies the phantom-like [maternal] Thing in me" (Žižek, *Enjoy* 144), and as such, for reasons related to the girl-child's separation from the maternal Other, which we will examine in more detail in the second part of this chapter, "the woman [is] more likely than the man to experience an uncanny doubling" (Copjec, *Imagine* 102).

As an index of the real, the Eskimo girl is undecipherable: she does not "mean" anything, but her presence affects, disturbs, unsettles, and compels Mary Jo in all sorts of ways, pointing to Mary Jo's betrayal of her own desiring self when she, Eskimo, "behaves as if she is confessing something – a shameful secret, a damaging mistake" (271). At that moment, she physically communicates to Mary Jo an experience of bodily jouissance: "She puts her fingers for a few seconds across Mary Jo's mouth [and] Mary Jo can feel the heat of her skin and the tremor that runs through the girl's fingers and her whole body. She is like an animal in an entirely incommunicable panic" (271). It is through Eskimo, this "word … that bothers" Mary Jo, this signifier of the uncanny, of the strangeness and familiarity of the self – "Fellow-Canadians," thinks Mary Jo (271), and yet a throwback to the past of the self –"'Inuit.' That's the word they use now" (271); it is through Eskimo that Mary Jo will encounter the fantasy that sustains her desire. In this sense, she speaks the truth when she suspects that, in her attempts to help the girl, she "may be seen as someone trying to get hold of the girl for her own purposes" (274).[4]

The real is not programmatic, and the encounter with it comes as a surprise, or as a shock.[5] After unsuccessfully attempting to isolate Eskimo from her partner by inviting her to meet up near the toilet, Mary Jo returns to her seat and encounters a sight and a look that penetrates to the core of her being. The sequence begins with Mary Jo's feeling that she "has caught something of the girl's persistent and peculiar agitation" (277), reaffirming the bodily connection between the two, and then Mary Jo's attention is captured:

> She cannot stop herself from watching what is going on across the aisle. What is going on is something she should have the sense and decency to turn away from. But she hasn't, and she doesn't.
>
> The girl has leaned forward and is kissing the man's face. His head is resting against the cushion and he does not stir. She leans over him, her eyes closed, or almost closed, her face broad and pale and impassive, a true moon face. She kisses his lips, his cheeks, his eyelids, his forehead. He offers himself to her; he permits her. She kisses him and licks him. She licks his nose … She licks him all over his face, then takes a breath and resumes her kissing … she is in a trance of devotion. True devotion … A ritual that takes every bit of her concentration and her self but in which her self is lost. It could go on forever. (277)

In this scene, Mary Jo encounters her own fantasy, which goes by the name of Eskimo. This fantasy masks the drive and protects the subject from the trauma of a direct encounter with that which cannot be symbolized as such, veiling it. The unconscious fantasy is never welcomed by the subject, as it exposes her subjective dependency on the Other; here it is one of devotion to a man. Interestingly, the scene reveals the two sides, male and female, of the sexual nonrelationship, a Lacanian formulation that does not deny the encounter of desiring bodies but emphasizes the fact that the fantasized "oneness" of sexuality does not obtain. Earlier, Mary Jo recalled the first time she and Streeter "made love" and commented on the fact that he shut his eyes: "He doesn't want to be reminded of himself at such times, and probably not of her, either. His is a fierce but solitary relish" (263). Here, in the fantasy scene, the man's eyes are also closed, but it is the woman who is involved in intense, solitary devotion. Jouissance, whether of the objet a (the woman for the man) or of the symbolic phallus (the man for the woman), is always solitary, notwithstanding the two involved and the consent given to each other (Brousse, "Sexual Position" 252).

What about the Other jouissance, that jouissance said to be feminine? In the Lacanian table of jouissances (*SXX* 78), man's desire reaches out to the objet a, located on the side of his partner: the side of woman. For a woman, one part of her jouissance in the sexual encounter is directed toward the symbolic phallus, which supports the man's being and is situated on the man's side of the table. There is therefore a jouissance that passes for each, through the encounter with the other, and in both cases, this is phallic enjoyment. In the fantasy scene of Eskimo, there is clearly phallic enjoyment involved, as Eskimo devotedly licks her man, making of him a full fetishized phallic object. But there is more, something that "is not wholly occupied with man ... is not, as such, at all occupied with him" (Lacan, *SXX* 87). In Eskimo's "trance of devotion," where "her self is lost," there are intimations of a form of limitlessness or infinity – "It could go on forever." This evokes the Other jouissance that Lacan theorizes in *Seminar XX*: that part of a woman's jouissance in which the drive does not involve the phallic signifier, but rather aims at the lack in the symbolic order, the breach in the signifying chain, symbolized, as we saw, by the gate held open in the story "Boys and Girls." It is a logical space, designated by Lacan as S(Ⱥ), which can be read literally as "the signifier of the Other which does not exist" or by its other name: the love letter. The jouissance of the love letter is a "supplementary" jouissance and, as such, is implicated in the sexual encounter, but in a particular way:

> This Other jouissance has a second side, which is not corporeal but discursive. It is a jouissance of speech, for it is a jouissance that includes love. Lacan does not situate love in the same place on the masculine and feminine sides. On the feminine side, love is part of jouissance ... And it is through the Other sex, through the woman side, that jouissance becomes civilized, through love, that is, through the inclusion of the Other in jouissance. The Other side is thus the feminine side. It is she who introduces the dimension of the Other with love. (Stevens 218)

It is in her love, in Eskimo's devotion not to her object, but to the Other-love in herself that is included in the sexual encounter, which in fact makes something of a "relation," that we can read the trace of feminine jouissance in this story. Thus, in her fascination with the scene of Eskimo's devotion, Mary Jo sees the fantasized form of her own desire: to love her man with a dedication that addresses through him both the phallus and the Other, and to have that devotion recognized by her partner as the "active gift of love" it is (Lacan, *SI* 276) by his consenting in turn to be the object of her love-desire, as Khan does for Eskimo – "He offers himself to her; he permits her." The woman who incarnates the *objet a* for the man finds herself in turn the *subject* of her own love-desire-jouissance.

This revelation of herself as subject of desire is not the end of Mary Jo's vision: "the girl's eyes open and she looks straight out across the aisle, with an expression that is not dazed and unaware, but direct and shocking" (277–8). At that moment, with the opening of Eskimo's eyes, the veil of fantasy is lifted. But "even then, Mary Jo has to keep looking" (278); she is frozen, like an animal hypnotized by headlights, and it is "only with a jolting effort, and after an immeasurable amount of time, [that Mary Jo] is able to pull her own eyes away" (278). Confronted by an image of the real, of unveiled jouissance, a hole opens up in her fantasy, dissolving its consistency. And since "the fantasy is the support of desire, [if] the fantasy collapses, so does desire. When desire collapses, the object becomes present, the object of the Other's demand, which indicates the certainty of jouissance. And we can start to see more clearly now that desire is a defense against jouissance, in that it introduces a significant distance between the subject and the object" (Voruz 168). Without this distance, the "certainty of jouissance," unmediated by the fantasy, invades Mary Jo. Watching the externalized and now unveiled expression of her own drive, desire slips away and she feels "sick with revulsion, as if she could feel the slow journeys of the warm, thick tongue over her face" (278). With nothing standing between herself and her drive, Mary Jo is overwhelmed by unwanted jouissance, so that "when she takes her eyes away, something else is released, and that is desire – sudden and punishing as a rush of loose earth down a mountainside" (278). The word desire throws us off track here, for Munro employs it in a context where what is presented is not the wanting or longing that characterizes desire, but rather an experience of lust, of unwelcome, bare jouissance, "that Thing insisting in her body as a 'tidal wave' of drive" (Bergeron 13).

FROM FANTASY TO THE DRIVE, FROM LOVE TO ... HATE?

This moment of jouissance provoked by an image of her sexual self immediately calls forth a disembodied voice, that form of the objet a that interpellates the subject in an imperative mode – it is the voice of Dr Streeter: "she is listening to Dr. Streeter's voice, and it says clearly, 'You know, that girl's teeth were probably knocked out. In some brawl'" (278). Coalesced in these imagined words attributed to Streeter are Mary Jo's object of desire (Streeter) and her phallic place of lack (teeth), as well as her fantasmatic double, Eskimo, through the reference to "that girl." The image is thus libidinally charged, so that the suggestion of "Eskimo" being "beaten" in a brawl points toward the erotic self-abasement constitutive of the fundamental fantasy of early childhood, whereby, in its attempt to know what the Other wants, the emerging subject positions itself as the object of the Other's desire, up to and including the possibility of its disappearance.[6]

Mary Jo attributes this position, that of the enjoying Other, to Streeter: "He is not just sad, not just accepting; he is satisfied that some things should be so. The satisfaction far back in his voice matches the loosening feeling in her body" (278). Hearing this "satisfied" voice of the Other, she hears the confirmation that the Other enjoys. The signifier "loosening" is significant here; metonymically carried forward from "the rush of loose earth" related to her earlier-mentioned landslide jouissance, it also signals libidinal pleasure elsewhere in Munro's writing. In both "Lives of Girls and Women" and "Royal Beatings," there is a question of libidinal discharge preceded by the word "loosen": Mr Chamberlain "loosened his belt" before a masturbation performance before young Del, and Rose's father's face "loosens and changes and grows younger," even as "his belt is coming off" prior to beating Rose.

For Mary Jo, the loosening in her body and the imagined satisfaction of Streeter are necessarily linked, thereby relating her desire to this fantasized other side of Streeter, and perhaps to the necessity that he take note of her phallic lack, symbolized by Eskimo's missing teeth, even at the cost of her violent disappearance. The image of the woman being knocked in the teeth is, in the symbolic economy of the story where much has been made of Mary Jo's dental work, hitting her where she exists as woman, a quasi annihilation of her being. Less a sudden insight into something new about Streeter, this is, for the protagonist, the recognition of an "unpleasant truth" about the functioning of her own desire: that in order to ensure that the other enjoys, she is willing to disappear (is that not what she is doing by going to Tahiti?).

Between hearing the voice and reflecting on its fantasmatic consistency, Mary Jo experiences shame: "She feels a physical shame and aversion, a heat that seems to spread from her stomach" (278). We note the repetition here of the word "aversion," used earlier to characterize her feelings about all the suckling children. But she also experiences "shame." This is not surprising if we accept that looking and shame are intimately related, as Copjec points out: "In the scopic drive, the subject does not see *itself* by looking at itself through the Other, but rather, in Freud's words … 'the self is seen in its sexual member.' It is this 'seeing oneself in one's sexual member,' in the exorbitant pleasure of the drive, that occasions the feeling of shame, of *being seen by others* as such" (*Imagine* 214, my emphasis). In looking at herself through the figure of Eskimo, it is as if the gaze of the Other, that obscure place in the mirror from which one can never see oneself, suddenly pierces through the eyes of Eskimo, revealing to Mary Jo that in her "looking" she is also "seen," seen in her sexual being. The moment is not a lasting one; the feeling of shame passes, "but the aversion remains" (278). "Aversion, disgust, dislike spreading out from you can be worse than pain. It would be a worse condition to live in" (278). The de-realizing modal "would" is already working to give Mary Jo some promise of distance from the unpleasant aftereffect of this invasion of jouissance. For, if shame is directed inwards, toward the self, aversion, in common understanding, is directed outward. The modal "would" seems to be an attempt to quell the aversion that is "spreading out."

Mary Jo then reflects on the experience of hearing Streeter's voice: she is aware of her own investment in the fabrication of this undercurrent of sadistic satisfaction in the voice of Streeter. The nuance that she "has put … into" his "familiar reasonable voice" has taken on the form of "a real delusion" for her, as something she "manufactured" so that she "could then turn away from [it], so purely hating him" (279). This hate of Mary Jo's, which is in some ways a measure of self-preservation, does not contradict her earlier-stated "permanent" love, so intrinsically are the two intertwined in *hainamoration*: this Lacanian neologism "is composed of the noun *haine* (hate) and the adjective *énamoré* (enamored)" (Lacan, *SXX*, Trans. note 90). Her hate is, in a certain sense, an index of her love. In other words, her love finds its hate "slope" because she sees all of the following in one fell swoop:

that she is Streeter's object, and that as such, part of his "satisfaction" is related to what she "lacks" in order to be this object; that there is an element of perversity in his fantasized objectification of her (registered in the satisfaction she projects onto him when she "hears" him comment on Eskimo / Mary Jo's teeth being knocked out,[7] but also to the extent that her work, and not her love, is being acknowledged). While she loves in him his giving over of himself as a heart doctor so long as he recognizes and values her devotion, she hates the part of him that sends her away, takes her away from *the place* from which she might be devoted to him. She can neither literally nor symbolically lick or kiss the face that has made itself absent. She cannot feel the return of the kiss.

Unsurprisingly, this rather astonishing moment in the story – seeing the self stripped of social consequence, at its ground-level, primary-signifier, Eskimo-level of desire, encountering jouissance through an unlimited devotion that passes through the phallic man – is not a welcome truth for Mary Jo. But there is worse to come.

We glimpsed the "beyond of fantasy" in the unveiling shock of Eskimo's direct gaze, a scene in which Mary Jo experiences a form of repetition of the very emergence of the subject: "The subject comes into being as a form of attraction toward and defense against a primordial, overwhelming experience of what the French call *jouissance*: a pleasure that is excessive, leading to a sense of being overwhelmed or disgusted, yet simultaneously providing a source of satisfaction" (Fink, *The Lacanian Subject* xii). The last part of the story will take this experience of repetition further still: no longer negotiated through fantasy, the story shifts to a more primal mode of expression – the dream. If fantasy gives fictional (fixional) form to desire, only the dream structure allows us to "approach the hard kernel of the real," the "point of failure of symbolization" (Žižek, *The Sublime Object* 48, 169), the place of what Lacan "calls, with reference to psychosis, 'perplexity'" (Guéguen 16).

We find here a way of going forward in the analysis of "Eskimo," for beyond the point we have reached, the narrative slips into the province of confusion, where images and words jostle and knock against each other, and a form of non-sense refutes any possible interpretative closure even as micro-metaphors emerge, dissolve, link up and become otherly, moving toward the point of perplexity that marks the place of the drives in their pre-symbolic encounter with language – in the *troumatic*[8] place of lalangue. The *mother* will not be absent from this space.

DRIVE

This last sequence of the story begins when Mary Jo falls asleep and starts to dream. The dream opens on some very obvious symbolism, whereby Khan gently pokes Eskimo with "the end of the furled umbrella" (279), while Mary Jo is still trying to get "the girl" to follow her to the "ladies' washroom." This time the girl follows. Keeping in mind Eskimo's function as the representative of Mary Jo's unconscious desire-drive matrix, we witness Mary Jo's resolve as she tries to get Eskimo to come clean: splashing her own face with cold water, she encourages Eskimo to do the same: "That's right. Cool your face off. Get your head clear" (280), and begins to speak to her "calmly and irresistibly," insisting that the girl say both what she is afraid of and what she wants, offering to get in touch with the authorities on her behalf. Is this a last ditch attempt on the part of the ego to bring the repressed (fears and desires) into a form of expression to which the Other ("authorities") might give their approval? "But the story halts at this point. Mary Jo has hit a dry spot, and her dream … translates this in its unsubtle way into an irregular, surprising patch of rust where the enamel has worn away at the bottom of the sink" (280). In its "irregular, surprising" aspect, this patch of rust is a place of dense associations: more than just the "dry spot" the text attempts to dismiss it as, it recalls, by colour association, the "rust-colored trousers" of the phallic Khan (267); as the place down and through which water flows, the sink with its "worn" patch of rust is structurally similar to Mary Jo's raw throat (265), which is the symptom of her uneasy desire; in its halting, "surprising" effect, the patch of rust also functions like the figures in the linoleum in "Royal Beatings" suggesting the presence of the gaze, the sign that the symbolic Other (the "authorities") is lacking, and therefore cannot provide coherence and meaning. Rust at the bottom of the sink also points in the direction of female sexuality, suggesting the menstruating vagina; the following phrase in the story puts in a "woman standing beside [Mary

Jo] at the next sink": "this woman covers her sink with her hands, as if she doesn't want Mary Jo to look at it or use it" (280). This spot is personal.

The "woman" becomes the next site of metonymic association: she is "a large, white-haired woman, wearing a red sari, and she seems to have some authority in the ladies' room" (280). She appears as a displacement effect of the Indian mother on the plane, who "wears a gold-embroidered red sari" (264). A mother figure, therefore.

At that point, "Mary Jo looks around for the Eskimo girl and is bewildered to see her lying on the floor. She has shrunk, and has a rubbery look, a crude face like a doll's. But the real shock is that her head has come loose from her body, though it is still attached by an internal elastic band" (280). In this image, Mary Jo / Eskimo sees herself as a thing, a "crude" thing on the floor in the washroom, the "badly maintained ladies' room," the domain of the woman in charge, the mother, at whose breast a baby sucks and lolls "with his eyes open," like Eskimo licking and kissing Khan, eyes open and staring into Mary Jo's. The association goes round, encircling the patch of rust at the bottom of the sink. This moment of "surprise," relayed by the "real shock" – that "her head has come loose from her body" – throws us back to an earlier moment in the story, when Mary Jo first complained of her raw throat and interpreted it as "her body … protesting its removal too quickly … from its place of habitual attachment and rest" (265).[9] Her thoughts at that earlier moment were focused on the familiar surroundings that she loved, because they were *her* surroundings, and which, by going to Tahiti, she was on the point of leaving: "This morning, she could see from her window a corner of Victoria park, the snow under the streetlights and the bare trees … the slushy streets, the dirty February snow, the gray walls of these houses, a tall office block with its night lights on, that she could see beyond the park. She wanted nothing so much as to stay" (265). Like the Eskimo / doll's body, separated from its head but "still attached by an internal elastic band" (280), Mary Jo is still secured by an internal bond / band to her place of attachment (she has not been fired, she is still a nurse in Dr Streeter's office), but she has been wrenched from it unwillingly, compelled by social expectations (the sadistic superego) to give her consent to abandoning her own form of happiness – a gray world set off by sparse but focused spots of light – in exchange for a travel brochure's substitute version of it.

But beyond this possible latent signification, the surprise – the "shock" – that accompanies the appearance of this image in the dream gives it the force of an unconscious knot: "the unconscious is only inscribed through ruptures, ruptures in sense and ruptures in the enjoyed [*joui*]… This is how the unconscious has manifested itself since Freud, but it took Lacan to remind us: through surprise … So the unconscious … is primarily of the order of encounter and revelation … Thoughts carry it, but it is primarily explosion, perplexity" (Guéguen 20). Mary Jo is, in this image of the ruptured self, the broken doll, brought back to her division as a subject, to her condition as a barred, lacking, internally divided subject. She is confronted by herself as a thing, as object, as objet a, as *a*bject, as waste, as unsignifying. It is her imaginary identification with Eskimo that has led to this reduction of the self to the objet a which is at stake in desire. As MacCannell comments, "The *object a* is always the center of identity and it is always consciously disavowed as that center: who, after all, would want to admit that something like a piece of shit lies at the center of his existence?" (131). When Mary Jo sees herself as broken doll object, she goes beyond an Other-dependent fantasy to encounter herself as drive, there where "the fantasy [ceases] masking the drive" (Miller, "The Sinthome" 64), or in other words, the point at which "*the fantasy becomes the drive*" (Lacan qtd in Miller, "The Sinthome" 64).

In the drive, there is jouissance, but no sense: Mary Jo's perplexity will only deepen before the opacity of meaning, as the woman / mother dream figure in the red sari gives her obscure injunctions – "You'll get a chance to choose your own" ("punishment" thinks Mary Jo) – then appears in different forms: in Streeter's office, as "a large figure entirely wrapped up in bandages (the Mother becomes a "mummy" to be fixed up by Streeter, who could have saved Mary Jo's mother), only to reappear in the red sari, conversationally both asking and affirming, "The court is in the garden?" This sends Mary Jo into a frenzy of interpretative stress: court of accusation, or court*ing*, or is it "count"? But then, *the* Count or "to count," and count what – his women?[10] Or is it a message about whether or not she counts for him? Meaning fails.

Court, says the woman, are flowers, "like *snow*drops, but blue" (281, my emphasis). Eskimo snow? The February snow under the streetlights? The mother-figure shows Mary Jo these flowers, bits of solidified jouissance in the form of blue snowdrops held in the palm of her hand.[11] These blue flowers are associated with the drives and desire through the conjoined signifiers "snow" and "drops," which create associations with Eskimo, with the cold water drops that refreshed her, and with the snow in the nostalgia-tinged streets left behind: associations cluster but do not create sense. Coming from the mother-figure, these words are decidedly, definitively enigmatic: Mary Jo will never know what the woman is telling her, or rather, what her "mother" means. All that is clear is the insistence of the mother's enigmatic shape-shifting presence and her place in the transmission of presignifying "letters."

Mary Jo is left bereft of meaning: the dream fades, and she "can't get back through the various curtains of the dream to the clear part, in the ladies' room, when the cold water was streaming down their faces and she – Mary Jo – was telling the girl how she could save herself" (282). Images of weeping, despair, and of persistent self-questioning flow together in this final image: the grammatical ambiguity of "how she could save herself" captures the constitutive doubleness that holds the Mary Jo / Eskimo couple in tension.

Her dream, like her fantasy, veils the place where the extimate real, the something beyond but intrinsic to the self, seems fleetingly within reach, and is gone. Mary Jo "can't get back" to the point of believing, expecting, or hoping that meaning, calculable and harmonious, instructive or transmissible, might be achieved. Her encounter with a fundamental aspect of her subjectivity, the real of jouissance poking through the fantasy veil, is now out of reach: it has returned to its habitual opacity. Like all those around her on the plane, "sleeping under blankets," Mary Jo is constitutively complex, irreducible to any singular meaning. Khan and Eskimo are returned to their status as others: as simply "[t]he man and the girl across the aisle," they are "asleep, with their mouths open, and Mary Jo is lifted to the surface by their duet of eloquent, innocent snores" (282). The place of the oral drive that has plagued Mary Jo throughout the story is seen gaping, but "reality" now veils it in "innocence." Mary Jo, too, is returned to the "surface" innocence of ignorance – the pulsating gap of the unconscious has closed again, leaving the reader in a state of uneasy confusion.

The story finishes on an ambiguous, if not provocative phrase: "This is the beginning of her holiday" (282). On the one hand, it appears to stand in for the absent explanation or meaning, supplementing Mary Jo's experience with a commentary. But the commentary is not one; the statement is neutral, purely factual, and creates a vacuum that invites narcissistic projections, or in other words, one can read it any way one likes. On the imaginary-symbolic (realistic) level, one might assume that this inner experience should necessarily end, deepen, revise, or in any case alter Mary Jo's relationship with Streeter. On a symbolic-real (fantasy) level, one might fathom this to be an ironic comment on what sort of relationship her desire compels her to accept and enjoy. On an imaginary-real (drive) level, having encountered herself in the fundamental fantasy "as desire's *objet a*," and having glimpsed the obscurity of herself as subject of the drive, a more original question arises: will Mary Jo's traversing of the fantasy allow her to decide whether or not she "wants what [s]he desires" (Lacan, "Remarks" 571–2)? This is not a question the story answers, but around which it circles, tracing out the contours of its shape, which is the shape of Mary Jo's being-as-lack.

"Too Much Happiness"

Feminine Jouissance

Like "Eskimo," "Too Much Happiness" is a story of travel – a train journey interspersed with memories. It is written in a dreamlike way, with an impression of uncertainty shaping the very syntax of the focalizing Sophia Kovalevsky's thoughts. Following the meanders of the story's journey, we will listen for its "other" knowledge and, along the way, give resonance to some of the echoes of this Other, feminine jouissance to which so many of Munro's stories bear witness.

"Too Much Happiness" departs from the Ontario-based fictional character typical of Munro's stories, taking as its protagonist the historical figure of the Russian mathematician Sophia Kovalevsky.[1] Kovalevsky's life is Romanesque in its outlines: born in Moscow in 1850, she excelled in mathematics but could not complete her studies in Russia, where women were not then permitted to attend universities. Nor could she leave Russia to study abroad without the permission of her father (an officer in the Russian army), or in the case of marriage, of her husband. As her father would not grant her leave, Sophia concluded a "fictitious" marriage with Vladimir Kovalevsky, a palaeontologist who would later become known for his work association with Charles Darwin, and the couple left Russia together in 1867. Sophia pursued her studies at the University of Heidelberg in Germany, and was later taken under the tutorship of reputed German mathematician Karl Weierstrass, becoming the first woman in Europe to hold a doctoral degree in mathematics. Her publications on complex mathematical problems earned her the reputed Bordin Prize, and she was eventually given a professorship at Stockholm University. In the meantime, her marriage with Vladimir (which took on more consistency than its original fictitious status had intended) had weathered his political engagement in the Paris Commune, the couple's immense financial difficulties, and the birth of their daughter Sophia (called FuFu). Indeed, it lasted until her husband's suicide in 1883.

Munro deals with these historical markers in gentle brushstrokes, allowing them to emerge progressively in the course of her protagonist's physical, reflective, and emotional divagations. The structure of this historical fiction hinges on a train journey: after walking in a cemetery on the first day of January 1891 with her new fiancé, Maksim Kovalevsky, a distant cousin of her late husband Vladimir, and referring to the ominous superstition that their presence in a graveyard on the first day of the year means that one of them will die within the year, Sophia boards a train.

The journey takes her from the sunshine, melting snow and "soft air" (254) of the south of France to the bitter cold and deep snow of Stockholm where she is to resume her teaching after the holiday break. The voyage will be interrupted by two detours: one to Paris to see her brother-in-law and her nephew, Urey, the only child of her now-deceased sister Ann; and one to Berlin to see her former tutor, the now aging Weierstrass. Each departure, arrival, encounter, and interval becomes an occasion for the emergence of Sophia's musings, recollections, thoughts, and feelings, and creates a tissue of connectivity around these disparate people and places, all of which strangely hearken to the past and to loss.

Indeed, it is a story that wends its way to death, as Sophia Kovalevsky will die of pneumonia shortly after her arrival in Stockholm. The train journey is thus a metaphorical visitation of her past and its marking moments, a taking stock of her life, her choices and possibilities as a woman, a musing over her loves and losses as death approaches. Indeed, death, announced obliquely in the cemetery – marked there in the image of the "melted black footprints" they leave in the snow (248) – and then forgotten, awaits her arrival, pulling her forward toward the cold and deepening snow, instilling itself into the narrative through the repeated references to a sore and worsening throat and fever. Aware of her symptoms – "she has time now to discover that she has a sore throat" (255) but not of their weighty meaning: "And her sore throat and slight shivers, surely a full-fledged cold coming on her" (268) – Sophia is not gloomy or self-lamenting. On the contrary, the breathless quality of the syntax, which employs few logical connectors and, quite unlike Munro's earlier writing, is sparse in its use of similes, creates a sense of a world freshly discovered, a world full of enigmas, not yet translatable, waiting to take on its meaning.

What is rather remarkable, in the context of the very different "reality" basis of the stories and the lives of the protagonists, is that the story, structurally, repeats the trajectory of "Eskimo." Apart from this sense of an expanding universe of potentiality in "Too Much Happiness," which contrasts with the sense of infinite regression and the final, baffled implosion in "Eskimo," much relates these stories written more than twenty years apart. Beyond the surface details of a woman on a train / plane, suffering from a sore throat, what is repeated, and what goes elsewhere?

WOMEN IN LOVE

In both narratives, the protagonist is travelling away from where her lover resides, consenting to leave but wishing to stay, resentful of the gift of freedom the man she loves is pressing upon her: Mary Jo is on a plane to a destination not of her choosing, resentful of being sent from her routine closeness to Dr Streeter; Sophia, newly engaged to be married, must return to her teaching but expresses a longing to stay: "How can I go, how can I leave this soft air?" (254). Instead of echoing Sophia's longing, Maksim reminds her of why she's leaving: "Ah, but your desk and your differential equations will be waiting. In the spring you won't be able to tear yourself away" (254). The circuitous quality of their conversation, which displaces their feelings onto the "air" or the "desk," clouds the tone and leaves Sophia uncertain about what is being said: "She must not think – she must not think that is a roundabout way of saying he wished they would not marry in the spring" (254). The reiteration of the imperative not to think carries with it the certainty that this is precisely one of the thoughts that will travel with her, making her feel somewhat stranded: "She spends the first hour or so of her solitary journey as she usually spends some time after a parting from him – balancing signs of affection against those of impatience, and indifference against a certain qualified passion" (255). Thus, she goes off, like Mary Jo, not with a light heart and certainty of her place in the other's affections, but tormented by the impossibility of discovering any certainty in the enigmatic words of her lover.

In terms that are not unlike certain passages related to Mary Jo's thoughts on Dr Streeter, Sophia reflects on what draws her to Maksim, trying to pinpoint what is specific to him as a man that attracts her:

> The marvellous assurance he has, that her father had, you can feel it when you are a little girl snuggled up in their arms and you want it all your life. More delightful of course if they love you, but comforting even if it is only a kind of ancient noble pact that they have made, a bond that has been signed, necessarily even if not enthusiastically, for your protection.
>
> They would be displeased to have anybody call them docile, yet in a way they are. They submit themselves to manly behavior. They submit themselves to manly behavior with all its risks and cruelties, its complicated burdens and deliberate frauds. Its rules, which in some cases you benefited from, as a woman, and then some that you didn't. (295)

In this passage, the difference between the position of a man and that of a woman in relation to the Other is one of obedience to rules, to the limit that, in the Lacanian framework, is necessarily the phallic limit that instates the function of castration. Men, in this view, are *defined* by the limit, whereas women remain undefined in this regard, except to the extent that their love, perhaps, *loves* that obedience to the limit in the man they choose. Within the sexual relation, as it is played out, the desire that supports this love of the man is for the symbolic phallus and is related to the phallic jouissance, which is one of the two forms of jouissance open to women in the sexual encounter.

The Other jouissance, supplementary to phallic jouissance, is envisaged precisely because a woman is not defined by the phallic exception: situated on the side of the not-all-under-the-sway of the phallic signifier, the metaphorical opening left in the symbolic universe gives her intuitions of a constitutive lack in phallic pursuits (all those pursuits that language gives rise to, all the attempts to "have" the something missing that would complete the universal masculine set. If the set is never complete, its idealized form nonetheless posits its completeness). The open set of the woman's side is incomplete by definition, and its incompleteness testifies to "the impotence of the signifier" (Copjec, *Imagine* 96). This failure of language, this lack in the Other, is unspeakable, but this does not prevent it from insisting as an intuition and, perhaps, as a shadow of that real of pre-language being associated with the maternal, since the maternal body, for a woman, is not only the mystery of where she came from but also of what she is, as unknowable to herself. As Copjec argues, the boy's separation from the mother is "simultaneous with an installation of the mother on the other side of a limit, in a paradisiacal beyond," whereas for a girl "that separation is not accompanied by an idealization." Rather, a woman, in her detachment from the mother, is "haunted by … a surplus, empty object … that forms as a result of her definitive, her radical giving up of the mother" (*Imagine* 101–2). This unknowable part of herself, this lack in the Other, written as S(Ⱥ), corresponds to feminine jouissance, to a real that weighs in on the symbolic dimension of a woman's universe[2] and finds its name in love: this is why what a woman "loses in losing love is herself, in the form of the named Other" (Soler, *What Lacan Said* 105). When she experiences herself as unloved, the haunting, surplus, unknowable, uncanny bit of real manifests itself in a woman in unpredictable ways. The Other whom she is, whom love "turns her into" (Soler, *What Lacan Said* 106) suddenly becomes unnamed, unnameable, adrift.

In both "Eskimo" and "Too Much Happiness," when love is in doubt, the integrity of the (named) self is threatened and reality becomes confused. A certain slippage in the very boundaries that define reality occurs, and the real seeps in through symptoms of sore throats and feverishness, signifying its bodily fixation; but there are also hallucinations, dreams, and a certain anxious perspective on the world seen as bereft of its usual stability of signs. Within the representation of sexed identity, this confusion of limits points to the woman's alienation in the absence of love: "Placing the cause of desire in the Other, [love] leaves the subject at the mercy of the caprices of the Other's response, and threatened with its absence" (Soler, *What Lacan Said* 102). In the absence of the particular other, of the other's love, the space left empty is invaded with *the presence of the lack of a limit*, the S(Ⱥ), which as we saw above, takes the form of an enigmatic mother figure – the Indian woman in the washroom in Mary Jo's dream. Similarly, in "Too Much Happiness," a familiar and foreign mother figure appears when Sophia's illness has become intense, her throat "so sore now that she is sure she could not speak if she had to" (293), and the environment, hostile: "On and on they go, through the dark, and there is something other than the snow driving against the windows. A scratching malevolent sound. Sleet" (293). In this context, "One woman" – one of the many foreign travellers bundled in "blankets and cloaks" – "took a fork out from a pocket in the folds of her clothing and ate pickled cabbage from a jar. That made Sophia think of home, of Russia" (291). This woman, who reminds Sophia of home, appears before her with a gift: "[She is] carrying two cups [of coffee] and it turns out that one is for Sophia. Sophia smiles and does her best to express gratitude. The woman nods as if this fuss is unnecessary, even unseemly" (294). The woman continues to stand there until "Sophia takes out the Danish coins ... [and] the woman, grunting, picks out two of them with her damp mittened fingers" (294). A symbolic transaction, an offering, but one that must be paid for – a debt and the hand-to-hand exchange of the symbolic payment – is accomplished here. This image then slips into another: "Some new passengers have got on. A woman with a child about four years old, one side of its face bandaged and one arm in a sling ... A hole in the bandage shows a sad dark eye. The child puts its good cheek down in its mother's lap and she spreads part of her shawl over its body" (294). The nexus of imagery in "Eskimo" – the mother figure or figures, the bandaged body, the presence of a child caught up in the mother's body / clothing, the hand revealing or offering an object that symbolizes a transaction, all of these are repeated here in "Too Much Happiness," taking us in the direction of the complex of mother / child that emerges in the thick of the woman's symptomatic uncertainty about love.

THE ENIGMATIC GIFT

There are differences, however. In "Eskimo," the mother's gift is not comfort, but an enigmatic message that confounds Mary Jo, leaving her caught within a wryly melancholic state where love and the question of guilt (as suggested by the references to "court" and "punishment," 280) become terribly entangled, leaving her with "an irreducible kernel of 'inconsolable' fixation on the lost being" (Soler, *What Lacan Said* 105) who is none other than herself *as* Other: "Let us recognize, in her trait of melancholy, [a woman's] attempt to speak of herself as Other" (Soler, *What Lacan Said* 104–5). "Too Much Happiness," however, does not spiral down into this melancholic grief. The Other that Sophia's feverish uncertainty gives presence to is "the other side of the phenomenon" (Soler, *What Lacan Said* 106): unencompassed by the phallic limit, she goes from love to Love, to the experience of a spreading outward of the loving limitlessness of what is sensed as the beyond of the symbolic universe.

Indeed, in "Too Much Happiness," the mother gives warmth and nourishment (the hot coffee) rather than jealously guarding her possession as the "mother" watching over her personal sink in "Eskimo" does, and she takes in payment only her due – "For the thought, and for carrying it, no charge" (294); moreover, she does not confound Sophia with enigmas. Sophia is not laden with a burden of guilt by the mother figure.

Instead, the advice, or message, comes from a man: a doctor encountered earlier on the train (a displacement of the Streeter figure onto a more benevolent position?). After chatting conversationally, one traveller to another, this doctor shifts his tone, and blushes, saying "I know who you are" (289) – a double-edged statement referring literally to his knowledge of her celebrity as a mathematician, and metaphorically to his understanding of her ills, needs, and desire. He talks confusedly of the scenery on the island of Bornholm where he resides, speaking of the "most *rare blue rock* … broken up and polished for ladies to wear around the neck" (289, my emphasis). Marie-Hélène Brousse refers to the fetishistic aspect of such objects as the necklace the doctor refers to: "Think of the interest girls show in small maternal objects, such as jewellery, shoes … objects that touch the female body … They serve to fulfil the function of the transmission of something feminine, which, through transmission, takes on the value of a symbol, or an emblem" (Brousse, "Qu'est-ce qu'une femme?").[3] This object "for ladies to wear around the neck" is mentioned as something Sophia might like to be given: "If you would ever like to have one –" (289). We are here reminded of the "small blue flowers – like snowdrops – but blue" in "Eskimo": unusual blue objects, associated with women and with the cold – the form of the enigma in these two stories, presented as an affirmation in "Eskimo" – "these are 'court'" (281), insisted upon as an imperative in "Too Much Happiness" when the talk of blue stone gives way to a plea: "Something I must say to you. It is not supposed to be spoken of. Please. On your way to Sweden, please do not go to Copenhagen. Do not look frightened, I am completely in my right mind" (289). And then he presses a gift into her hand, not the blue rock but its metonymic displacement, "a small tablet" to give her "a little rest [should she] find the journey tedious" (290). The doctor has informed her that there is an epidemic of smallpox in Copenhagen, a piece of information never certified in the story, and there is no way of ascertaining whether the roundabout route he suggests has any literal function or not. The journey is treacherous, her condition worsens, she hardly knows which country she is in, and she is at pains to get her body to where it needs to be. Running to catch another train, "She ran lurching and panting with a pain in her chest and around under her arms and the bags bumping against her legs … With tears of self-pity filling her eyes she beseeched the train not to move" (297). It is only once she has boarded the train, "laughing with triumph in between spells of coughing" (298), and is on the last leg of her trip, that she takes the tablet given to her by the doctor.

The tablet is a miracle pill, a pain reliever that removes the limit that pain throws up between self and other, but more than that, metaphorically, this tablet removes the very notion of boundary, so that an unprecedented, incomparable "extraordinary feeling" goes "rippling through her" (298). Suddenly, comparisons abound. Everything is "as if" or "like": "as if her heart could go on expanding, regaining its normal condition, and continuing after that to grow lighter and fresher and puff things almost humorously out of her way" (299); it is like "her first stumbling on trigonometry, when she was twelve years old … she was able to break into this new and delightful language. She was not very surprised then, though intensely happy. Such discoveries would happen. Mathematics was a natural gift, *like* the northern lights. It was not mixed up with anything else in the world, not with papers, prizes, colleagues, and diplomas" (299, my emphasis). This rippling happiness, discovered but not sought after, received but not transmissible, the unexpected gift, an illumination of the sky,[4] which is entirely unconnected with anything else, gives us an inkling of the fleeting experience of the Other jouissance.

On the brink of death, Sophia merges into the Lacanian angel-being, the *être-ange, étrange, strange* shape of the gap between the symbolic and the real.[5] Lacan evokes the spider's web as a metaphor of the material manifestation of this gap: "It is a truly miraculous function to see, on the very surface emerging from an opaque point of this strange being, the trace of these writings taking form, in which one can grasp the limits, impasses, and dead ends that show the real acceding to the symbolic" (*SXX* 93). The spider's web metaphor allows us to visualize the process of meaningless markings (the real) taking logical shape (the symbolic). In an inversion of this process, we see Sophia becoming the strange angel-being that bridges the gap in the other direction, going from the symbolic to the real, using the signifier to attempt to spin out a text to bridge the gap to the place where the Other is lacking, where meaning dissolves. When Lacan evokes the angel, he refers to its smile as *bête*, which is rendered as "stupid" in Fink's translation. This seems appropriate because the "beast" that *bête* refers to is an animal-being outside of language, and the etymology of "stupid" includes associations with "stunned," "dazed," or "confounded." In both cases, meaning is blocked. Like the Lacanian angel, stupidly smiling because "it is up to its ears in the supreme signifier," Sophia is radiant with all forms of happiness – she is "too full of glowing and exceptional ideas to speak to people any longer" (300); she resists the empirical cold because of "the enchantment in her mind and body" (300), and in her deathbed confusion and elation she speaks about her new vision: "There was a movement back and forth, she said, there was a pulse in life. Her hope was that in this piece of writing [the one she planned to undertake] she would discover what went on. Something underlying. Invented, but not. What could she mean by this? She laughed. She was overflowing with ideas, she said, of a whole new breadth and importance and yet so natural and self-evident that she couldn't help laughing" (302). Sophia dies in the wake of this delirium, her last words caught with uncertainty by one of those close to her: "Teresa thought she heard her say, 'Too much happiness'" (302). The paradoxical gift is her vision of a happiness that would be "too much," an overspilling of uncontainable joy, glimpsed at intermittently in her life, but somehow also outside of life's ebb: an ecstasy to be borne in small doses, received sporadically as a gift from life itself, but that cannot be sustained in the engulfing, symbolic-effacing excess of the "too much."

INTIMATIONS OF OTHER JOUISSANCE

"Eskimo," I have argued, finishes on an enigma that traps Mary Jo within the field of "reality," leaving open the question – What is she going to do with all that she feels? How can she live with the enigmatic, concentrated jouissance of the snowdrops, shown by the m(Other) in the beyond of fantasy, an unwanted selfhood as abjection that sustains her very mode of desire and therefore her place within the symbolic and social world? "Too Much Happiness" asks a different question – Can Sophia live within the expanding Other jouissance of lack, transported outside the symbolic world of limitation and constraint? – and answers No, linking this all-encompassing jouissance to her impending death. To be tolerable, Other jouissance can only be "occasional and fleeting" (Fink, *A Clinical Introduction* 99).

Such "fleeting" moments, which do not advance the plot, which do not inscribe the characters in their social universe, but rather illuminate their singularity by revealing the breech whereby the wondrous invades the commonplace, are numerous in Munro's writing. They ground her stories in "the freedom of a great unemotional happiness" that escapes causality and leaves open the door to welcome the "miracles" of the "other country" (Munro, "Dance of the Happy Shades" 222, 224).

In "Too Much Happiness," Munro takes further an earlier and enduring preoccupation: to find the words that might suggest, but never exhaust, the value of these fleeting experiences of rapture: "I felt able to cope with everything. I really felt so buoyed up, so excited, by this writing thing that I had latched on to. It gave me in those years the most enormous happiness. I was quite stunned by what I was able to do, at fifteen or sixteen. It's just that way of being able to translate a kind of rapture that I think everybody feels – the thing is to find a way of expressing it. And I really felt able to do that then" (Munro, qtd in Tausky). Whether everybody feels that kind of rapture or not is an open question. Freud comes to mind here; he gives credence to the "oceanic feeling" evoked by his friend Romain

Rolland, "a feeling as of something limitless, unbounded – as it were, 'oceanic,'" all the while affirming that he, Freud, could not discover this oceanic feeling in himself (Freud, *Civilization* 1–2). Soler has linked this oceanic feeling to the Other jouissance that Lacan theorizes as a possibility emerging from the non-limit on the feminine side of being, a "jouissance that does not fall within the discontinuity and short duration of phallic jouissance and does not call for a complementary object of lack" (*What Lacan Said* 171). In Munro's writing, this sentiment is recurrent, and sometimes seems to be a product of an openness of disposition. In "The Turkey Season" (*The Moons*), the young female protagonist is walking to work in wintertime, and observes:

> There was the Turkey Barn, on the edge of a white field, with a row of big pine trees behind it, and always, no matter how cold and still it was, these trees were lifting their branches and sighing and straining. It seems unlikely that on my way to the Turkey Barn, for an hour of gutting turkeys, I should have experienced such a sense of promise and at the same time of perfect, impenetrable mystery in the universe, but I did. Herb had something to do with that, and so did the cold snap – the series of hard, clear mornings. The truth is, such feelings weren't hard to come by then. I would get them but not know how they were to be connected with anything in real life. (68–9)

The mention of Herb, a reassuring male presence at work, links this pleasure in the universe to the human, and to sexual difference, without allowing that to become sufficient to explain the experience entirely; something about this "sense of promise" remains unconnected to "anything in real life." It emerges elsewhere in the fissure of the end of a love relationship: "When you start really letting go this is what it's like. A lick of pain, furtive, darting up where you don't expect it. Then a lightness … There's a queer kind of pleasure in it, not a self-wounding or malicious pleasure, nothing personal at all. It's an uncalled-for pleasure in seeing how the design wouldn't fit and the structure wouldn't stand, a pleasure in taking into account, all over again, everything that is contradictory and persistent and unaccommodating about life" (Munro, "Bardon Bus" 127). The "furtive lick of pain" that links the body to the experience of life as "contradictory and persistent and unaccommodating" and finding pleasure in this bodily affirmation of being, both before and after all plans, projects, and hopes, even of love, have come to naught, might also be a figure of this feminine Other jouissance.

I have already noted that a woman's jouissance in the sexual encounter includes love, but this jouissance "is not wholly occupied with man, and … is not, as such, at all occupied with him" (Lacan, *SXX* 87); rather, it belongs to the feminine stance, which excludes nothing from the all of experience, and which, precisely, can therefore never be gathered up into an "all." In "Circle of Prayer" (*Progress*), a woman hears her mother-in-law playing the piano, a dance piece that seems out of place and character, and later remembers the moment: "She sees her young self looking in the window at the old woman playing the piano. The dim room, with its oversize beams and lonely leather chairs. The clattering, faltering, persistent piano music" (372). Here the reader senses the effect of this remembered vision, that of the older woman seen by the younger woman, suggesting that something important but intangible about the lives of these women is being carried falteringly on the notes of music. The women, who are clearly separate and isolated (metaphorized by the window, by the separating dimness), are nonetheless connected by the son who became the husband, by the passing of time, and by their openness to the unexpected:

> Trudy remembers that so clearly and it seems she stood outside her own body, which ached then from the punishing pleasures of love. She stood outside her own happiness in a tide of sadness. And the opposite thing happened the morning Dan left. Then she stood outside her own unhappiness in a tide of what seemed unreasonably like love. But it was the same thing, really when you got outside. What are those times that stand out, clear patches in your life – what do they have to do with it? They aren't exactly promises. Breathing spaces. Is that all? (372)

Excessively intimate, and yet "not personal at all," not entirely communicable, breaking into the symbolic world but never assimilable within it, never assignable to one side of the structuring binaries, never countable, Other jouissance remains outside the circuit of exchange. Yet Munro allows for the possibility of glimpsing the presence of this "openness to the lack in the Other" in some "others" who are often figures of marginality, those who, for their pleasure or pain, are differently situated in the social field. *Lives of Girls and Women* finishes on such an *apercu* when Bobby Sheriff, the local "lunatic," home from the asylum for a rest, invites Del, the young protagonist, to "step into [his] yard and try a piece of cake" ("Epilogue: The Photographer" 272). As they sit chatting amiably, Del wonders: "There must be some secret to madness, some *gift* about it, something I didn't know" (275). Then, as she finishes her cake and he "relieve[s her] of [her] fork, napkin and empty plate," he says to her:

> "Believe me [...] I wish you luck in your life."
>
> Then he did the only special thing he ever did for me. With those things in his hands, he rose on his toes like a dancer, like a plump ballerina. This action, accompanied by his delicate smile, appeared to be a joke not shared with me so much as displayed for me, and it seemed to have a concise meaning, a stylized meaning – to be a letter, or a whole word, in an alphabet I did not know.
>
> People's wishes, and their other offerings were what I took then naturally, a bit distractedly, as if they were never anything more than my due.
>
> "Yes," I said, instead of thank you. (276–7)

Reworked from a point in the future, the memory of this balletic gesture and the smile displayed for her younger self nourishes the narrator's understanding that there are private "letters" that do not belong to shared language, whose meaning cannot be exhausted by the signifier, or by the interpretive gesture, and that this knowledge is a *gift*. Like Eskimo, a word both strange and familiar that becomes unmoored from its referent to suggest, but not "mean," the opacity of Mary Jo's desire, or "too much happiness," the paradoxical proposition of the excessive plenitude experienced by Sophia, these dedicated attempts to make the reader feel the rapture of being-in-lack or of lack-in-being are enigmatic gifts, like the little bits of blue rock or snowdrops planted in the stories, to be passed on, hand to hand, as intimations or reminders of the transformative openness of language, and its beyond.

"Tell Me Yes or No"

The Love Letter

While desire and jouissance were at the centre of the analyses in the previous chapters, here, in my reading of "Tell Me Yes or No," it is love that is in question. A narrative situation is given in which a woman is in love with a man, and more than that, she has made the irreversible choice of *this* love, *this* man. At the same time, she doesn't believe in her luck: the unexpected encounter, the declaration of love, the heady promise (and weighty determinism?) of a shared future. The unfathomable desire of a man for a woman; can it be durably sustained as *onelove*? Or will he be a serial lover, constantly yearning for one *more* woman, leaving her abandoned? This is the anxiety that structures the doubled story in "Tell Me Yes or No" where Munro scrutinizes love up close: from the first "glimpse" (108), to love's declarations, through the question of choice and the evocation of the social forms of love's expression, the question is painstakingly pursued. This includes taking into account the fundamental misunderstanding between the sexes that complicates and sometimes undoes love.

Structurally, the story follows two intertwined threads: the first presents a woman's fantasy of her lover's death and the second, her remembering of the beginnings of their love story. These threads are laid out in the first lines of the narrative as the woman's thoughts address her lover:

> I persistently imagine you dead.
>
> You told me that you loved me years ago. Years ago. And I said that I too, I was in love with you in those days. An exaggeration. (106)

Two openings therefore, through two disconnected statements, where the disconnection is marked in the text by the difference in layout: the first line is flush with the left margin, the second indented. The first is a death fantasy in the present tense; the other inaugurates a reminiscence of a time long ago, when a time yet further in the past was evoked, a time that becomes blurred, slipping almost into the indefinite temporality of fairy tales (Ventura, "The Setting Up of Unsettlement" 112): a time when love was spoken of.[1] Then, to counter the temptation to fall into the sentimentality suggested by the tightly knitted "I's" and "you's" comes a statement of ironic deflation: "An exaggeration." This revision of the emotional density of the declaration of the past gives a possible tone of bitterness to the present of enunciation, suggesting a certain coherence between a suffering love and a death fantasy.[2]

It would therefore be easy to read the story, as some critics have, as a negation of love and its illusions, and the death fantasy as retaliation for the loss of love (Carrington 109; Ventura, "The Setting Up of Unsettlement" 121, 122). I would argue, however, that the story's paradoxical structure needs to be embraced: while the fantasy concerns, even *proposes* the death of the lover, it does not express, in any pure form, a wish for him to *be* dead; it is a fantasy that includes the possibility of unrequited love yearning for the annihilation of the lover, but on the condition that he can be resuscitated. In this sense, it explores a hypothesis: *Your love for me remains an enigma to me, something uncertain and beyond my control, and yet my very being has been captured by you because I love you. Therefore, only your death can set me free from the anxiety of uncertainty. By imagining you dead, I can imagine myself having survived the loss of that part of myself that is now yours.*

FALLING IN LOVE

Having offered two threads to follow, the narrator begins with the love strand, telling the story of the couple's relationship: she and her lover first met in the 1950s, they both lived on campus, were both married, and she was mother to a young daughter. One day, after a chance encounter, they found themselves heading for "that wild, partly wooded patch of land above the river" (108), the symbolic landscape of obscure and flowing desire. In spite of the "tension" they felt, they "never touched each other" and the encounter ended there. Or not entirely: "Next day, or the day after, when I was reading as usual on the couch, I felt myself drop a lovely distance, thinking of you, and that was the beginning" (109). The contingency of an encounter in its incalculable effects is conjoined here with the response of the body to a nascent desire, represented as a feeling of "dropping," or falling in answer to a glimpse of "what more there could still be" (109).

Is this love? Not yet. Nor is it simply a reaction to a hypothetical frustration in the narrator's own couple, along the lines of the "desperate housewife" image of the 1950s. For the narrator, this too would be an exaggeration. At that time, in her marriage, she "felt nothing so definite as dissatisfaction," and she dismisses any facile mockery of the clichéd images of the period: "Too easy and not the whole truth, because it leaves out something that was appealing, I think, in our heaviness and docility, our love of limits" (107). The appeal of the phallic satisfactions of motherhood, of the security of married life, and of the associated prestige of the husband's professional ambitions might figure in this evocation of "something appealing." Perhaps also, the freedom from tension – from, precisely, jouissance. Commenting on Freud's theory of the pleasure principle, Lacan remarks: "The pleasure principle ... is nothing other than the principle of least tension, of the minimal tension necessary to be maintained for life to subsist. This demonstrates that, in itself, enjoyment [jouissance] goes beyond it, and that what the pleasure principle maintains is the limit as regards enjoyment [jouissance]" (*SXVII*, 14 January 1970). This love of limits, of the orderly life, of accepting that past intimations of the "sin and splendor" of sex have "shrunk to this brisk, unvarying, satisfactory, localized exchange" (107) is indeed one version of the pleasure principle, and the narrator will continue to live this life, with some satisfaction, for an indefinite but consequential number of years.

Later (two years prior to the present of the narration) comes the second chance encounter: she was divorced; he lived in a distant city and was still married. They fell in love. He fell first and then she did. What is this love into which they fell? It begins with speech, with putting into words the trace of that possibility glimpsed in the past. On the part of the lover, this takes the form of a love declaration, one that addresses something in the woman that she does not recognize in herself. She reminisces, "I remember sitting at lunch with you, and when you said, 'I loved you. I love you now,' I looked past you at myself in the restaurant mirror, and I felt embarrassed for you. I thought, God knows why, that you were being gallant, I did not take the words seriously, and I thought that in a moment you would look at me and see that you had said this to the wrong person, to a woman who had abandoned the whole posture, the vocabulary for dealing with such tributes" (111). Supported by his desire, the lover, in declaring his love, makes of this woman his beloved. Yet what Munro's text brings out is the sense of mistakenness experienced by the beloved, by the woman, who does not recognize in herself the object of desire that has captivated the man. It is "beyond" her. Knowing all about the feminine masquerade of seduction and the romantic language of love, she feels that there are codes that she has forsaken and that make her alien to that "vocabulary," ineligible for the role of the beloved.

What is the inscrutable lovable something in her that prompts the man to bring love into existence by naming her as his beloved? It is her lack. Once again, the lack-in-being of the feminine position of subjectivity, which is not locatable per se, since it is in excess of the phallic-symbolic order, is the place from which love emerges.[3] In love, it is this being as virtual non-being that is at stake: "This 'being' at stake for both the lover and the beloved, is, in the final instance, a lack-in-being, which is a way of saying that in love, the enigma of what I am to myself is always involved, as well as that of what the other is for me" (Hoornaert).

The woman first encounters this enigma in the form of the man's declaration of love. Although, initially, she doesn't take it seriously, she subsequently affirms: "Then I understood that you meant what you said and it seemed to me more than ever that you must be mistaken" (111). The woman is being offered this man's love, but love is also "giving what you don't have – your lack – to someone who doesn't want it" (Lacan, qtd in Hoornaert).[4] The man is offering his lack, making himself "poor" for her so that their two lacks might meet: the subjective destitution of the love declaration implies making oneself vulnerable, to such an extent that she feels "embarrassed" for him, and initially at least, she "doesn't want it." Moreover, the woman is surprised by the offer and finds it difficult, almost preposterous, to believe that she, seeing only a negative lack in herself, should be offered this gift of love.

A CHOICE: FROM CONTINGENCY TO NECESSITY

At its outset, therefore, love is an unlikely affair: an unexpected encounter between two lacks. Nothing necessitates love, as the woman points out: "Love is not in the least unavoidable, there is a choice made. It is just that it is hard to know when the choice was made, or when in spite of seeming frivolous, it became irreversible" (111). Munro captures here the transformative nature of the experience of love: from the unexpected to the necessary. From a love that "stops not being written" to a love that "doesn't stop being written" (*SXX* 94).

"Tell Me Yes or No" sketches out the movement of this transformative experience, retracing the words spoken and what they might have meant. This "I loved you then" of the man, proffered two years prior to the present of the narration, what can it have meant? She considers the question: "You say you were in love with me and I reply that I was in love with you, but the truth was surely different. More likely, we got a glimpse of something, through each other, that we had not been thinking about – had put aside, in your case, or not yet discovered, in mine" (108). Love is at first a possibility glimpsed; nothing that binds.

In *her* version of their story, the advent of love, understood after the fact as involving a choice, took place on "a freeway" as the sun was setting on a day in November. The moment is intensely charged symbolically and brings together two good omens: a positive sense of being understood by her lover-to-be, and a sign of encouragement from "the universe" itself. The first comes just after the man's suggestion that she delay her departure from the city so that they might share a night in a hotel. The woman hesitates: "'I don't know. No, I don't think I can. I'm too tired.'" He replies, and then she does: "'I am not so strenuous.' 'No.' We were holding hands all the way, in the car. I freed my hand and made a gesture meaning I was tired of something else – experience? – I was not sure what I meant myself but expected, rightly, that you would understand" (112). In Lacan's view, "Love is an obscure recognition … [from] 'enigmatic signs' of the way in which the other is affected by the destiny that the unconscious has made for him" (Soler, *Lacan* ch. 17). This gesture of the hand that is suddenly "freed" gives fictional form to the enigmatic sign, and the man's "understanding" of it points toward this aspect of "recognition." Following Miller, "love is addressed to the one you think knows your true truth" ("On Love"). It is a relation of subject to subject, an encounter between two lalangues – two languages of the unconscious. In this way, "the mystery of love is not reduced, but [is] linked to its unconscious foundation" (Soler, *Lacan* ch. 17). Moreover, love understood in this dimension is an imaginary relationship that does not pass through the Other (the superego, the law). Whereas desire is supported by the fantasy objet a, love, this "new love" of Lacan's, has no mediating object. It is outside of social discourse, and aims at the "being" of the other, at the obscure place where her knowledge of herself is, to herself, unknown: the place where her being emerges from its constitutive lack. In this dimension, "when one loves, it has nothing to do with sex" (*SXX* 25). Love, the encounter between two lacks that recognize each other, is "outsidesex" or "beyondsex" (*SXX* 85).[5]

The woman's sense of having been understood precedes "a turn" taken in their journey so that, "coming off the access road," facing west, she sees before her the earthly equivalent of a divine blessing: "The streaks of the sky between the clouds were a fiery pink. The light of the cars seemed to stream together, mile after mile. It was all like the kind of vision of the world, a fluid, peaceful vision, utterly reassuring – that I used to get when I was drunk. It said to me, why not? It urged me to have faith, to float upon the present, which might stretch out forever" (112). This encouragement from the sky, from a universe suddenly suffused with good omens of a love that might bring together space, time, and beauty, contributes to, and at the same time confirms, a choice in the making, one that is underlined by the poetic coherence of the passage, where the *s* and long *e* sounds of "streaks," "seemed," and "stream" alternate with the *ai* of "sky," "fiery," "light," and "mile." The rich imagery of the sky, the light, and the evocation of peace and faith create a positive, spiritually connoted "vision," one that is perhaps not prophetic but holds a promise: that of conjoining the "present" with a form of "forever."

But what can "forever" mean in terms of earthly love? Even the span of a lifetime is denounced in our skeptical times as impossibly limiting for any human love. Alain Badiou takes up the challenge of defining "eternity" in love: beyond the initial encounter, the declaration of love inscribes love's contingency "into the framework of eternity," "it is an anticipation of eternity"; "that's what love is: a declaration of eternity to be fulfilled or unfurled as best it can be within time – eternity descending into time" (47).

We can rephrase this as a shift in modalities: from the mode of the contingent to that of the necessary. The "always" of the love declaration is not an always of chronos, it's a modal eternity: a way of living the now that includes the necessary, the symptomatic, something beyond the pleasure principle. It becomes – and this is the meaning Badiou gives to "fidelity" – "the movement from a chance encounter to a construction that is as solid *as if* it had been necessary" (43, my emphasis). It is not, as the story points out, an "unavoidable" transition, and is therefore dependent upon a "choice" which, like that of sexuation,[6] is an unconscious one, and which therefore remains partly obscure to the protagonist – "Was that when the choice was made, do you think, when I saw the sky and the car lights?" (113). The "you" in this phrase reminds the reader that this reflection on love is ostensibly addressed to the lover, and concerns the questioning of their relationship; in fact it interrogates what the other thread of the story develops: the discordance in their approaches to love and desire. I will come to that thread further on, but this reminder of the existence of the other, the "you" who is her lover, reinstates the fact that this questioning of "what love is" cannot be dissociated from the disharmony between the sexes: "Love comes as an illusion to the place of the sexual relation that does not exist. But love has to pass from contingency to necessity. Love as necessary, as decision, can then produce a substitute – which is not the same thing as an illusion – for what lacks of the sexual relation. It is no longer simply an illusion, for one shifts from the imaginary to the symptom" (Stevens 218). Love becomes the subject's symptom and demands repetition – *encore*: hence the "irreversible" nature of the choice that the woman affirms; there is a before and an after the knotting of the subject to this love-symptom, irrespective of the fate of the love "story" as it unfolds in that "after."

In the argument developed above, it may seem that two propositions are in conflict: that of love as "inter-recognition" of two subjective unconsciouses, and love as an illusion or symptom covering over a fundamental disharmony. How can there be disharmony in a context of such fundamental empathy? Perhaps it would be useful to reread the quote from Stevens: in its inception, before the choice that makes of love a symptom, "Love comes as an illusion to the place of the sexual relation that does not exist." Here the inter-recognition implied in love is an illusion; it aims at what can be extracted as "sameness" and is inscribed in the romantic tradition. The two who meet, in spite of their "infinite subjectivities" – which Badiou argues must be preserved to form the basis of a "Two Scene" that gives love a chance of flourishing – the two who meet, then, are often drawn toward a conception of love that seeks fusion, that attempts to make of the two a "One Scene": "This is love conceived of as fusional: the two lovers meet and something like a heroism of the One makes its stand against the world" (Badiou 30, translation modified). This form, this discourse on love, in which the lovers feel destined or fated to be together is a persistent Western myth and finds its inscription in European literature and popular culture, and most often ends in death.

Contemporary disillusionment with love may owe much to a romanticism that was always doomed since based on an impossibility: no illusion of sameness, no "inter-recognition" between the two, can ever efface the otherness of the other, which includes the misalignment of the positions of desire implied in the jouissance(s) of a man and of a woman.

VERSIONS OF LOVE

If "eternizing the present" of love requires a shift from the contingent to the necessary, this leaves open the question of the fictional form, or implied model of relationship, that the lovers will adopt: love looks for signs, for signs of how to love, which are always historical, espousing the myths of the day. For Lacan, these myths of love are important as they "give epic form to what is operative at the level of structure" (*Television*). What myths of love were available in North America in the 1970s, the time in which the story is set and which is also the place-time of its writing? What signs would it have been possible to give? Was it the love of the One Scene or Two Scene: fusional love or a meeting of subjectivities? Traces of various, contradictory myths are inscribed in the story: courtly love, free love … new love?

Courtly Love

In the protagonist's reception of the man's declaration of love, she disbelieves him, thinking he was "being gallant," paying "tributes" through choice "vocabulary" (111), all of which, as I mentioned earlier, make her "embarrassed" for him. The "being" of "being gallant" is not equivalent to an essential trait; rather the progressive aspect of the verb points to its transitoriness. He is "acting" according to codes, and her embarrassment suggests that this performance is either unseemly, anachronistic, or both. This does not prevent her from later declaring, in a positive appraisal, her perception of a "chivalric" quality in him, and even her own self-consciously overstated insistence that he *embody* the courtly ideal: "I do expect you, like a knight, to be capable of acts of outmoded self-sacrifice and also of marvelous brutality, both performed with the kind of style that indicates obedience to secret orders" (116). The word "outmoded" needs to be underlined here; the woman knows that such expectations belong to a vanished world, one that Lacan comments on in his seminars, pointing out the astonishing historical fact of the appearance of the courtly love tradition: "It is truly the most amazing thing that has ever been attempted." Lacan describes courtly love as "a highly refined way of making up for the absence of the sexual relationship, by feigning that we are the ones who erect an obstacle thereto" (*SXX* 69). This tradition includes the establishment of the woman as the object, not only of desire, but more importantly, of the man's faithful devotion, in spite of the impediments to attaining his goal. The exceptional woman is the One, not the One of fusion, but the One who stands precisely *as* the exception, an ideal, the One against whom all others pale in comparison. The Lady of courtly love is the clearest historical form of the Woman as the embodiment of an unfathomable mystery, the Woman whom Lacan declared does not exist. To that extent, the model of courtly love might best be seen as a *form* of Two Scene, but one that fixes the roles of each, and by reifying the "infinite subjectivities" of the partners, makes of love a dead thing.

Free Love

In reality, there was very little force left in the courtly model of love in the 1970s world of sexual liberation; there was no time for, or patience with, the inaccessibility of women or the multiplication of obstacles. For the narrating woman in the story, her present world is peopled by others – men, but also women, like her by then-adult daughter – who seem to embody free relationships, "moving ... as smoothly as eels among their varied and innocent and transitory loves" (106). There is no explicit value judgment on this new generation, which is already worlds away from the domestic ideals of her early married self of the 1950s; yet the word "eels" with its predatory snake-like connotations adds an ironic touch of evil to the portrait of these "innocent … loves." It is, in any case, not a model she that she dwells on, certainly not one through which she views her own new love. In this model of love, there is no "two," just an infinite number of interchangeable "ones"; here, contingency never makes the shift to necessity. Indeed, love is not in play at all, since the being of the other is never in question; it is a model of relationship in which jouissance holds the key role, and as Lacan points out, "*Jouissance* … is not the sign of love" (*SXX* 4).

New Love

Luck exists and so does love and I was right to go after it.

Munro, letter to Virginia Barber in Thacker, *Writing Her Lives* 289

Contemporary society is at pains to find a new suit for love, one that might fit our present-day reality which, as Soler points out, is "unfavourable to myths of love" (*What Lacan Said* 215). If Lacan's version of love is to be understood as subjective inter-recognition that takes into account, or *aims* at the very being of the other, it is on the one hand a minimalistic myth that leaves much scope for invention on the part of the couple, but it is also one that requires the recognition of one's own lack as the condition for a readiness to be caught up in the enigma of the otherness of the other: it requires a leap of faith. As a proposition, it effaces neither of the lovers, and preserves the "two" in love. Beyond that, everything remains open.

"Tell Me Yes or No," in the love story strand of the text that I have been following, takes the woman to the point where different models of love in circulation are acknowledged. She herself, we have seen, uses the metaphors of courtly love to signify that she wants her man to be "like a knight" with the corollary that she, for him, should be the idealized Lady, his mysterious "one and only." And yet, unlike traditional tales of courtly love, there are no obstacles on her side to this knight errant's access to her: *she* is divorced, *he* is married. In a sort of inversion of roles, he is the one whose accessibility is restricted, emphasized in the story by his residing in a distant city that she has never visited. He comes to her, seemingly at will, while she is forbidden access to him. Since the reality effect of the story is weak, as neither characters nor places are named, and cause and consequence are only minimally present, is this physical distance a metaphorical device indexing the fact that something of her lover, and his love for her, remains unfathomable and inaccessible to her?

The woman situates herself a generation away from the new generation of "free lovers," but she is in no way surprised at the man's suggestion that they spend the night at a hotel, and she accepts the proposition. Not for jouissance alone, for she is "tired," in a vast and general way. It is on the basis of the urging of the fiery sky, and the intuition of an "understanding" between them that she makes the leap of faith that engages her on the path of love, not nameable as such, but proclaimed nonetheless: "We both trembled. We barely managed it, being overcome, – both of us, both of us – with gratitude, and amazement. The flood of luck, of happiness undeserved, unqualified, nearly unbelieved in. Tears stood in our eyes. Undeniably. Yes" (113). Conjoined here, in love and sexual jouissance, is amazement, happiness, even joy at the good fortune that befalls them "both." If the word love is absent from this passage, it is inscribed in the line that follows, a reflexive comment on that moment: "If you had been a man I had met that day, or at that time in my life, could I have loved you? Not so much" (112). The love revealed in that moment is welcomed as an "undeserved," "nearly unbelieved in" sort of miracle.[7]

THE FAULTY DECLARATION AND THE MISSING PACT

What can make such a miracle, the miracle of a bond of love, exist over time? The simplest answer to this is "words": "There is no love that begins without a declaration, no love that subsists without words" (Hoornaert). Love requires speech, and the ideal form of the declaration is "I love you," rewritten by Roland Barthes as "I-love-you," a "holophrase" that supports no variation, no social constraint, no nuance ("Fragments" 176–7): it is not informative, it is an unpredictable and irrepressible cry from the heart. What is the status of the declaration in

"Tell Me Yes or No"? The man, we have seen, declares his love in the following way: "I loved you. I love you now" (111). What can be said about this love that is restated ("loved," "love") and situated in time (past tense, then "now")? Is there continuity or discontinuity in this past and present love? What about tomorrow? There is promise, but also uncertainty in this declaration, which does not have the force of an *unqualified* "I love you," the only form that infinitizes the present of love.

Beyond the opening declaration, and its instances of reiteration, love must also find its social insertion as a pact between the lovers. The function of the pact is to refer the love of the couple to a "sacred" value outside of the individuals themselves, to something that is not entirely defined by their individual wishes, hopes, and feelings, and not entirely encompassed by the limits of the law. The traditional form of the pact is, of course, marriage. Where religious marriage includes the reference to the sacred, civil marriage demotes the pact to the status of revocable contract, but still (potentially) includes the value, beyond the individuals, of the inscription of their love in the permanence of the social order as such. In "Tell Me Yes or No," there is a pact, but it is not between the man and the woman narrator; it is between him and an "other" woman: his wife. Consequently, in the death fantasy aspect of the story, the narrator notes that their relationship was largely hidden from the public eye: "Nobody knows I have lost anything, nobody knew that part of my life, except in a general, rumoured way" (110). Without the pact to write their love in the social script, what can assure the woman that she is the one, his one true love?

For, in Hoornaert's reading of Lacan, "Love gives value to one woman that differentiates her from all the others. Whereas desire, by definition, slips along from one object to another, love stands as an objection to this metonymy … Love makes of its object the aim of desire, and no longer a means to its satisfaction." Without the formal promise that the pact signifies, how can the woman free herself of the anxiety that she is just one more stopover in the metonymic movement of her lover's desire? What can assure her that *he too* has made the "irreversible" choice of love?

LOVE'S ANXIETIES: THE FEAR OF FALLING

Nothing can provide this assurance in an absolute way for any couple, and while marriage covers over or veils the fundamental doubt that love includes, it does not eliminate it. If love demands love, to the extent that every demand addressed to the other includes a demand for love,[8] the response to that demand needs to repeatedly hit its mark; and yet, love, "as it presents itself in modern times, misses the being of the other" (Hoornaert). Indeed, a woman who seeks confirmation that she is loved in a way that is "necessary" to the other is in a precarious position:

> Love, unfortunately, is risky and ephemeral, as we have always known. This is why it aspires not to cease being written; it wants to elevate itself to the necessary.[9] Exalting when one succeeds in encountering it, love is also depressing when it is lost. Placing the cause of desire in the Other, it leaves the subject at the mercy of the caprices of the Other's response, and threatened with its absence … Women more frequently [than men] make love into a cause, and when it is missing, either contingently or through the acts of civilization … they are left stranded. (Soler, *What Lacan Said* 102)

In "Tell Me Yes or No," beyond the initial recognition and moment of mutual loving – "both of us, both of us … Undeniably. Yes" – there is nothing but uncertainty.

The uncertainties of love find their inscription in the story through a modulation of the idea of "falling." After "dropping a lovely distance" (109), a phrase that emphasizes the pleasantly unsettling effect of the promise of love, the narrator later notes, "I loved you for linking me with my past, with my young self … If I could kindle love then and take it now, there was less waste than I had thought. Much less than I had thought. My life did not altogether *fall away* in separate pieces, lost" (113, emphasis mine). The love of this man, known in the past, loved later on, gives fictional unity to her sense of self, experienced as fragmented, but in the reflecting mirror of the man's love "then" and in his love "now," a gathering up of the self, an echo of the mirror phase of imaginary wholeness, is produced. But just as the subjective unity of the child in the mirror is an illusion, the perceived unity of the self produced in love is also precarious, all the more so as the man in the story does not seem to rely on the woman for *his* self-image, and will not cultivate the myth of himself as a heroic knight: he sees himself as "genial, corrupt, ordinarily selfish and pleasure-loving" (117). To her repeated demands that he disclose some word that would reveal him to her and reassure her that his love for her is unquestionable – "I desire revelations" (116) – he laughs and reaffirms his view that there is no mystery, no secret behind his love, or indeed beyond life: "what more could there be?" (116). This absence of any transcendental aspect to their love bond deepens her uncertainty into a pervasive fear: "As if this hole I *fall into*, which is the permanent absence of you, is nothing but a dream I scare myself with" (117, emphasis mine). The syntax and temporal structure of the phrase make its status undecidable: how far does the "as if" extend? Does it modulate the value of "permanent" within the fantasy narrative? I understand this "as if" statement to be indicative of the knot of desire and uncertainty that is the very symptom of the story. This fear of falling is the fear of losing love, and it gives rise to the fantasy in which it partakes.

The story pursues its love strand in a minor mode, overshadowed from that point on by the present-tense passive-aggressive fantasy of the lover's death, within which it is entirely subsumed and which constitutes an attempt to conjure away the anxiety of new love. This anxiety is related, as I have suggested, to the fear of its disappearance, and is given symbolic embodiment through the character of the lover's wife who functions less as a specific "other woman" than as a generic reminder that the man's attachments are not wholly given to the heroine: she is a part of his desire, but she is not all to him; he has other obligations. While the anxiety of being abandoned is clearly at stake in the fantasy, we should also note that there is another side to the anxiety of love: Soler points out that love, especially for a woman whose love – the giving and receiving of – becomes the very *cause* of her desire, can also be a burden. The sense of the preponderant, perhaps overwhelming place love will now occupy in the life of the woman as beloved is difficult to bear: "Love … can by its very presence overwhelm the subject with the weight of an Other; what makes the weight even more crushing is that the cause of desire is attributed to the Other: Freud recognized this, emphasizing that love and melancholia are two cases of being 'crushed by the object'" (Soler, *What Lacan Said* 102).

This leads us to the death fantasy, which allows the woman to express both her fear of abandonment and, to a certain extent, her wish for it.

"I PERSISTENTLY IMAGINE YOU DEAD"

The woman's memories of the emergence of love in the couple she forms with her married lover are intertwined with references to the fantasy that he is dead. Within this fantasy, a past is composed, one that involves his visits (at intervals that are not defined in the story) from the city where he lives with his wife, and between these visits, an exchange of letters takes place. It is impossible to say what part of the past situated within the fantasy structure (the present-tense narrative) corresponds to a "reality strain" in the narrator's life. Is the structure of the relationship (a distant one including the "other woman"-wife) real, or is it part of the fantasy?[10] It would be simplest to accept this as part of the reality level of the story, but the unlikely introduction of another "other" woman later on – a patent "double" figure for the narrator – calls verisimilitude radically into question. Rather than trying to ascertain what is "real" and what is fantasized, we will simply accept that the fantasy is "true" in that it encodes in fiction the unconscious questioning of the narrator, even as it addresses, in the form of an appeal, her lover.

What does this fantasy of the lover's death say about love? To begin with, it writes into the love relationship that which constitutes the fundamental obstacle to it: the disharmony between the sexes, which follows from the different ways in which they are situated in relation to symbolic castration, and the differences in their modes of jouissance. Unlike a man's structuring fantasy, which pursues an obscure but necessary object and includes the dream of a "One"-ness through union with that object, a woman's sexual fantasy includes the desire to be loved, and the "One"-ness she dreams of is, to some extent, dependent on extracting a portion of the man's fantasized Oneness to supplement her lack, or leave her less alone with her radical *Otherness to herself*, by naming it with the name of her love(r). Soler writes, in this context, of

> the specifically feminine call for a chosen love. This requirement will not be able to resolve the disharmony of jouissances; rather it will repeat their disunion, which in bringing the sexes closer together, gives existence to the absolute Other, making woman always Other: Other to herself. Love therefore will not leave her

> alone with her *heterity*, but will … index it with the name of the lover: such is the case with Juliet, made eternal by Romeo, Iseult by Tristan, or Beatrice by Dante. What can be deduced from this is that for a woman, the loss of love exceeds the phallic dimension to which Freud reduced it, for what she loses in losing love is herself, in the form of the named Other. (*What Lacan Said* 105)

The fear of loss of the self is fundamentally at stake in "Tell Me Yes or No," all the more so, one might argue, as neither the narrator nor the lover are named. It is a fragile symbolic world into which their love is inscribed, and his "name" is already taken. On what will she be able to index her need for a chosen love, one that guarantees her place as his One? The anxiety to which this uncertainty gives rise is not assuaged by their exchanges: on the contrary, their discussions only emphasize the dissymmetry of their expectations in the relationship: "You would look over your glasses at me like some mild inflexible schoolmaster, put out by my extremity. We would have to consider my being in love, the way I am in love, as if it were a curable extravagance, a highhanded assumption in an essay" (116). The question of the "way" the narrator is, in love, is picked up on in the following paragraph where she affirms that she "knew this was a dangerous way to live" (116). What exactly she is referring to through the demonstrative pronoun "this" is uncertain: is it the prospect of entering into a relationship with a married, only intermittently accessible, man? Or is it more fundamentally the very prospect of giving herself over to love, of trading the evenness of her position as "a woman who had abandoned the whole posture" of desire for the heady prospect of a river of love figured as "stream," "fluid," "flow," "flood," and "creek" (112–14), but with the risk of drought, where love leaves her heart "cracked … it is dry and cracked like a bare bit of landscape marked with gullies" (117). This is the risk that the fantasy of her lover's death explores: If I love, and love is lost, will I survive?

The theme is recurrent in Munro's work: in "Simon's Luck" (*The Beggar Maid*) the fear of losing love dominates the narrator to the extent that, because of one missed rendezvous, she presumes that love has deserted her, or if it hasn't yet, it inevitably will do, and so she leaves everything, including her home and her job, to force a form of certainty (of absence) on a situation of uncertainty (of presence), the latter being unbearable to her. In "Tell Me Yes or No," which is anterior to the writing of "Simon's Luck," the death fantasy is the way in which the narrator opens up a space of certainty – the certainty of the loss of love – so as to explore what it might mean to her: Would his death, the death of his love, also mean the drying up of life for her?

The fantasy is a hysterical one in the sense that it addresses her lover as the one who is supposed to be able to "tell her,"[11] that is, as the one who is presupposed as holding the answer to the uncertainty that riddles her. This fantasy begins with a question – "Would you like to know how I am informed of your death?" – and targets the metaphorical site of love: "A *heart attack*, that will do" (109, my emphasis). It is then worked out around the symbols of the love letter, the letter box, and the Other woman.

LOVE LETTERS

What was I, in the end, writing for you? The only thing one can write that is a bit serious – a love letter.

Lacan, *SXX* 84

The exchange of letters is a recurrent feature in Munro's stories, most of which are set in a time prior to the expansion of computer technology, when even a long-distance phone call was a notable event.[12] What characterizes the exchange of letters is, above all else, absence. The written word, the words on the page, the page itself, the enveloped leaf of paper, stand in for an absence that is the missing presence of the writer. What necessitates this absence? In "Tell Me Yes or No," the lover's absence is due to his other commitment: his wife. But this wife, like Streeter's drunken wife in "Eskimo," is desexualized, castrated in terms of her potential as a rival: "She doesn't dance any more. She had an operation on her knee" (111). She is a commitment from the past, an obligation he must attend to. She is also a device, an "invention," the word with which the narrator will clear away the story and all of its fictional attributes in the final paragraph. The invention of the wife serves to imagine the incarnation of an obstacle to the fantasized fusion that love would ideally bring about, as attested by the vision of the fluid streaming together of all things that the narrator experienced as the intuition of a love to come. If it does not "come together," there must be a reason: the wife, as the fictional support for the failure of love to accomplish union, provides a rational explanation or pretext for a structural impossibility. Lacan notes, "The epithalamion [nuptial song], the duet … the alternation, the love letter, they're not the sexual relationship. They revolve around the fact that there's no such thing as a sexual relationship" (*SXX* 57). Love letters "revolve" around the impasse of the fantasy of fusion, shaping the contours of its rim or lip. Thus, the fantasy frame sets up an exchange of letters: first his to her, and later, hers.

HIS LETTERS

The letters from her lover are structurally present from the beginning of the fantasy. No sooner does she kill him off than she mentions his letters and the place they occupy in her life, which is that of a fetishized object:[13]

> I am in the habit of carrying around your last letter in my purse. When the next letter comes, I replace it, I put it with all the earlier letters in a box in my closet. While it is fresh in my purse I like to take the letter out and read it at odd moments, for instance if I am sitting having coffee in some little café, or waiting at the dentist's. Later on I never take the letter out at all, I grow to dislike the sight of it, folded and dog-eared, reminding me what weeks, what months, I have been waiting for the new letter. But I leave it there, I don't put it in the box, I don't dare. (109–10)

The sexual symbolism underlying the passage is evident: the letter-object appears as the phallus, the signifier of a desire addressed to her, which she puts in her "purse," a typical representative of feminine sexuality. The object functions metonymically, one letter replacing another, love's demand (*encore*) receiving a flow of objects, renewing the signs of love. The content of the letters is not discussed; it is their function as objet a that matters, their function as representatives of the surplus jouissance of love and desire conjoined. Metonymically renewed, they are also metonymically displaced from one feminine container to another: from the "mailbox" to her "purse" to a "box" in a "closet" where her lover's letters accumulate. The end of the process is announced in an instance of grammatical ambiguity in the first line of the quotation above: "I am in the habit of carrying around your last letter in my purse. When the next letter comes ..." The word "last" falls into the place where "latest" would be more likely, since more letters are to follow in this time frame of the habitual. But the truth is pushing forth in this misplaced word, for the truly *last* letter is pending; it has, in fact, already arrived.

"Knowing" he is dead, that there will be no more letters, no more exchange, no more love from him, she puts his last letter away. Whereas previously, she "did not dare" to take the "dog-eared" sign of his love out of circulation, she now does so: "I go home and remove this letter, this last letter, from my purse, put it with the others and shove the box out of sight. Deliberately, almost painlessly I do this" (110). If we accept that "[on] a symbolic level, the circulation of the letter itself assures that it has already reached its destination, the Other or the symbolic" (Rabaté, "Psychoanalysis Applicable" 63), by putting it "out of sight," she takes his love letter out of the symbolic. But she does not destroy it. It no longer belongs to the sphere of the symbolic, but it remains tucked away in her "closet." Thus, we encounter the letter not as an external, symbolic object, but as an intimately exterior or ex-timate, real object: the letter as libidinal trace.

Before focusing on this aspect of the letter, I'd like to linger a moment on the textual density of "boxes" here. With past letters preserved *in* the box *in* the closet *in* her home – or in other words, in the recesses of her intimate space, the other box – the public one, the mail(male)box, visited by the intermediary of the postal agent, will henceforth remain empty, becoming the sign of "no love." Like the not quite negated pain in the phrase "*almost* painlessly" above, pain persists in the text, as the narrator tries, consciously, methodically, insistently, to rid herself of it: "Every day when I come back from teaching I see the mailbox and to tell the truth I experience something pleasant, a lack of expectation. For two years that tin box has been the central object in my life, and now to see it go neutral again, to see it promise and withhold nothing very much, that is like feeling a pain gone" (110). The writing here captures the paradoxes of the woman's effort to hold herself together, to explain to her lover (whom she has positioned as dead, but still "listening") that she might experience his death (i.e., the death of their love) as a relief of sorts, as it would allow a return to the *absence of tension* (the tension of expectation) that Freud, as we saw earlier, defines as the pleasure principle. Thus she envisages the "lack of expectation" as a "pleasant" prospect, even as the ritualistic "every day" negates the absence of expectation she is trying to affirm, under the guise of the not quite convincing "to tell the truth." Similarly, the whole paragraph circles round this empty box, the metonym of her desire, "the central object in [her] life," affirming and denying its effects by delaying the negation in "promise and withhold *nothing*," "feeling a pain *gone*," rather than using the more usual "not … anything / anymore" to frame the verbs. The tension of ambivalence is forcefully felt here as the woman invents a version of herself as one who is no longer the receiver of her lover's letters.

THE QUEST

In the fantasy framework of the woman's narrative, what comes after the "end" of love is a pilgrimage to the place where the lover lived, a journey that reveals itself to be a quest, a search for knowledge about herself, and about how to recover the part of herself that her lover had in his possession: she goes, unknowingly, to recover her letters. This is announced to her lover as a visit, in a formula that, through the simple and perfect forms of the present tense, keeps him alive, even as he is dead (or the contrary): "As soon as the term ends, in late April, I mean to go to visit you, to visit the city where you *have died*" (111, emphasis added). Why do people go to the place where someone lived and died, after their death? Is it the need to encounter the place where meaning circulated and stopped, where the relationship found its final expression, its ending? Is it to perform a ritual that would serve as a burial to the personal, imaginary hopes entangled in the life of the other person, to recuperate that possibility of hope for oneself, to be able to go on? Munro deals with this question of travelling to the place of the "dead" lover obliquely: the narrator goes to his city, not to look for his grave, but for traces of him, and ultimately for his widow, the other woman.

Since she does not know this, or where she is going, her travels begin with a strong sense of disorientation, where the unfamiliar streets present themselves in a discordant jumble of sights and sounds as she walks "everywhere," where light is "dazzling" and the flowers so colourful they "hurt the eyes," where the mixture of architectural styles ranges unhistorically from modern "filling-station style" houses with flat roofs, to buildings with "misplaced portholes," by way of "Tudor teashops" and cave-like shops "from which issue recorded jungle noises" (115). In the midst of this onslaught of false fronts and phony appearances, she fantasizes the encounter of her image and his crossing in shop windows, but like the misaligned architecture, which emerges out of no historical necessity other than commercial gimmicking, their reflections miss each other. He was there, he lived there but is "dead"; she is alive but out of place: the rendezvous is *manqué*, which she knows even as she relates this effort to find in these streets "some memory of you." As the dream is always about the dreamer, what she can encounter here, in this fantasy space, is not him, but herself: "Windows which hosted your reflection give me back mine" (115).

MAP

Becoming more purposeful in her search for her path, the narrator announces, "I have bought a map" (117),[14] thereby expressing a desire for guidance and direction. Following the logic of her loss, she looks for and finds her lover's street easily enough, and then, his house; she confronts the possibility of looking into the "house you never meant me to see" – in other words, the place that is most intimate to him: the correlate of her own closet. This possibility of knowing her lover's secret self is, to the narrator, a risky prospect. Even within the fantasy structure that supports it, she distances it further: "Imagine this real, a real house, where people wash dishes and oversleep. At night if she doesn't draw the curtains I can look into your rooms. Are the pictures your choice, or hers? Neither. Both. These discoveries cause me ordinary pain" (118). The imagining, the possibility not actualized – "if," "can" – and the indeterminacy of (expected) result – "Neither. Both" – indicate her reluctance to pursue this temptation. What is there ever, in Bluebeard's closet, when a woman looks into it, but other women? She does not want to confront the other woman there where he lived, but rather where he is dead. She goes to look for his widow.

PHONE BOOK

The expression "the other woman" is used in everyday language to refer to the mistress of a married man. Here, the gist of the expression goes in the opposite direction, since the "mistress" goes to look at, be near, and wonder about, the one who was her lover's wife. This inversion includes a deflation of the expected emotional connotations: this other woman is not a sexual rival. I argued above that she is, to a large extent, desexualized, and serves in the fiction as an imaginary obstacle to explain the impasses of the narrator's relationship to her lover.

Unlike looking in her lover's house, going to see his widow is something the narrator decides that she "can do" (118). Without difficulty, she finds the professional address of this woman in the phone book, under B for Barbara's Book Mart (118). To what end? What can this lacking woman tell her? Does she go there to ask her something? Not at all; rather, she observes her, tries to see what she has or is such that, in spite of her granny-like appearance – "Her hair is gray, grayer than mine, pulled into a bun" (118) – the man stayed with her. Moreover, the comparisons, inaugurated in the syntagm "grayer *than mine*," slide into a general picture of a woman who, like herself, had "abandoned the whole posture" of seduction (111); "no make-up," "she is a stocky middle-aged woman" (118–19). The effect on the narrator of being near this woman, whom she "knows" – "I know her at once" (118) – is filtered through the focus on her voice:

> She goes behind the desk, puts [the books] on a shelf, speaks to the salesgirl as if continuing a conversation started earlier. "Well, I don't know how – *invoice* – phone them up and tell them that isn't the way we do things around here – whole damn lot's got to be returned."
>
> I remember her *voice*, the same *voice* I heard all that time ago at one or two parties – a clear challenging *voice* that seems to come into its own on a certain level of exasperation, a *voice* that excels in saying *My God what are those idiots thinking of!* Suppose she remembers my *voice*, or my face? (119, my italicization of *voice*)

Introduced through the signifier "invoice," itself separated from the flow of the sentence by dashes, the *voice* suggests a link to the past ("remember," "all that time ago") and, in some way, to an ongoing "conversation"; the iteration of the word *voice* gives it privileged status, that of the invocatory partial drive that functions in the imperative mode (as noted in relation to the voice of Streeter intruding on Mary Jo's thoughts in "Eskimo"). This authoritative woman is capable of settling accounts, of making sure that things unpaid for are "returned." She is clearly related to the repetition of the drive, that of the narrator; we see the woman progressively taking on the recurring Munrovian function of the unconscious double.

At the level of the latent content of this fantasy, the narrator's observations and comparisons move toward fascination as she comes to the shop "day after day," the better to "listen," "hear," and once, to receive a look and a smile (120), so that the woman becomes the image of a fantasized significant Other, leading the narrator to the dominant sentiment in Munro's work: shame: "I can imagine becoming her friend, *listening* to her confidences. I am ashamed of such a fantasy. I feel envy in her presence, and a precarious triumph, and this frivolous desperate curiosity; I am ashamed of all this when I remember" (120). Here there is envy, triumph, curiosity, and shame. This Woman elicits both phallic competition – *who* did the man really love? – and something beyond it, something related to knowledge about desire, and the way these questions return the subject to her dependency on her mortal sexed existence and the extent to which she is determined by this obscure jouissance. The desperate curiosity of the narrator becomes an obsessive fascination that questions this Woman: like herself, this widow has suffered the loss of the man, but she seems to have retained her subjective consistency – she is not "ashamed." Does this Woman have the answer to a man's desire?[15]

Anxiety runs through the narrator's (imagined or actual) exchanges with her lover, anxiety that she has failed to occupy the place of his desire, has failed to give the right answer to a question that she presupposes in him. In love, feminine anxiety concerns this uncertainty: "Her [a woman's] anxiety is only before the desire of the other which, when all is said and done, she does not know very clearly what it covers" (*SX*, 20 March 1963).[16] In the only transcribed epistolary *exchange* between the lovers, anxiety is present on both sides. The man signifies to the woman that there is something *excessive* about her, that threatens him, and the woman both denies and confirms his knowledge:

"*I do think of you I suppose as a warm and sentient flood, you wrote one time to me, and I have the normal human concerns with being overwhelmed, which is what floods do.* I wrote back that I was nothing but the tamest little creek you could go wading in. You knew better" (115). The desire to correspond to some undefined, implicit expectation on her lover's part, one that involves not loving too much, leads the woman to conceal her love, to downplay it: "Half my concern in love became how to disguise love, to make it harmless and merry" (114–15). The strain produced by the effort this requires might explain the general sense of being "too tired" for a new relationship, a sentiment that the woman had put forward in the prelimen of their love.

What can appease the anxiety related to the uncertainty of the other's desire? One response is to see a man's desire as contained within the man himself; such desire is not dependent on the woman, on what she does, how she appears, or how much she loves. This structural response to love's anxiety gives rise to the feminine fantasy of the Don Juan figure: "Paradoxically, a woman finds an answer to her concerns about men's desire and their phallic power in the fantasy of Don Juan which, as Lacan points out, is essentially a feminine fantasy[17] … For women, this fantasy proves [or gives form to the wish] that there is at least one man who *has it* from the outset, who always has it and cannot lose it, meaning that no woman can take it from him" (Salecl, "Love Anxieties" 96; my emphasis). The casting of man as Don Juan would therefore reassure a woman that, in his serial gathering of the women needed to make up the complete set of women,[18] he is unshakeable in his phallic desire; he cannot be castrated. The woman who, through the bond of love or marriage, is associated with such a man does not count herself among the "collectibles"; she is, in her own view, the named exception: "Her 'special' properties make her see herself as one-minus on the list, and not as just one more … By 'counting' this way, women can have it both ways. She sees that a man makes a list of women that may include her. But by believing herself to be 'unique,' 'not all' under the symbolic rule, she can exempt herself from the list and see herself as the one held outside, the transcendental one" (Ragland, "The Woman Not Seen"). In this way, the woman can become the Ur-Woman capable of sustaining the desire of the serial lover; he can have the others, but he can never *have* her: she is the exception that is not affected by the metonymy of his desire, nor can her specific qualities undermine his desire, which is seen as his essential quality.

Consequently, it is not really a question of desire between them: the Ur-Woman occupies a place from which the man's desire is seen as sustained, but he finds the objects of his desire elsewhere. Is this not the position attributed to Barbara of the Book Mart? As desexualized wife, she is the unshakeable, never negotiated point of attachment for the man. In this sense she is Woman for the man and a point of identification for the narrator, an introjection of what would be necessary for the protagonist to be certain that her lover's desire cannot fail, that he will not be castrated in his desire for her.

THE OTHER FACE OF THE OTHER WOMAN

There is more to this Woman. The etymology of the Christian name Barbara, through its Greek and Latin origins, associates it with the idea of the foreign, strange, barbarous, or alien. This exotic, otherwordly personage (dressed, incidentally, "in a faded purple smock with bands of Indian embroidery" (118), likening her to the Indian mother figure in "Eskimo"), opens up the space of the Lacanian "Other" Woman who, mythologized as mysterious, enigmatic, whole, and powerful, does not exist, but whose very real impossibility marks the place in the symbolic order where meaning both fails and proliferates. This is the place of the S(Ⱥ), the signifier of the barred Other, the opaque place where "Woman, if she existed" (*SXX* 82) would be situated, a place from which a jouissance not bound to the signifier (not located in the law and its transgressions, nor in the symbolic-imaginary and its fictions) emerges, not as a definable "existing" something, but as the point at which symbolic and imaginary productions both originate and collapse.[19] This place is that of lalangue, where the signifier has left its mark, as jouissance, but not its meaning; as the *lettre-jouie*, deposited bits of jouissance tied to unchained signifiers, it constitutes the treasure house of "our potentiality for being."[20]

This Other Woman, Barbara, signifies this *extimate* place "to which woman is fundamentally related" (*SXX* 81); for the narrator, whose being is sexed in the feminine mode, and not therefore having been called upon in her encounter with the symbolic law to embrace difference *away* from the mother, as the boy is called upon to do, her being remains penetrated by a vague jouissance of heterogeneity *to herself*, which is the trace of the m(Other) in her, not as an incomplete separation from the actual mother but as an effect of feminine sexuation. The Other Woman is the Lacanian invention, which accounts for the fact that "the woman lives herself – enjoys her body – as if it were not her own but another's, as if she were the double of another" (Copjec, *Imagine* 102); this double is *not* the mother, but the manifestation of the fact that feminine sexuality involves a jouissance experienced as "a disruption of self-identity" (Copjec, *Imagine* 103). For Lacan, love recognizes this Otherness of a woman, includes its possibility (Soler, *What Lacan Said* 106).

When the narrator goes to the city of her lover, it is therefore to visit the opaque place of jouissance to which she is fundamentally related, as the space outside of signification (*horsens*) that needs to be encountered in any act of creative invention: to reinvent herself after the end of "this love" she needs to find herself, not as a signifier within the symbolic, but as a letter in the real, in the unconscious space of lalangue. She goes there, paradoxically, to *return* to her own desirousness through her encounter with the Other Woman, since this other woman holds the letters, not of her meaning, but of her being. The voyage may now to be seen as a quest to have her letters returned to her.

THE RETURN OF THE LETTER

Having passed through an imaginary identification with the wife figure, who is her age, looks like her, and yet incarnates, by being other than her, her non-identity to herself, the narrator is directly confronted by Barbara. This woman, to whom her unconscious is related, knows the truth and speaks it: "I think I know who you are" (120). The "content" of this knowledge is contained in the bag of letters she gives to the narrator, who goes away with them: "In my apartment I open the bag and take out the letters. They are letters, not in their envelopes. That is what I knew I would find, I knew I would find my letters. I don't want to read them, I dread reading them, I think that I will put them away. But then I notice that the writing is not mine. I start to read. These letters are not mine, they were not written by me.

I skip through every one of them in a panic and read the signature. Patricia. Pat. P. I go back and read them carefully one by one" (120–1). Misrecognition is a fundamental aspect both of the narrator's relation to Barbara and to the Patricia of the letters. Whereas the classical form of misrecognition in the imaginary is to suppose that you are the intended addressee of the message of the Other (Žižek, *Enjoy* 12–14), that is, to recognize yourself where you are not, here it goes in the other direction: she does *not recognize* herself in these other women, who hold and write the letters of her being – in other words, they are constitutive of her self, as unknown to herself.

This nonrecognition of what, in her, ex-sists, is not only understandable, but necessary, since "the unconscious is a paradoxical letter which *insists* only insofar as it does not *exist* ontologically"; it is the very "'condition of the possibility' of the letter that it must be overlooked, that we must not take notice of it – its very existence depends on its not being seen by the subject" (Žižek, "The Truth" 200). So, while the narrator does see the letters, she "overlooks" the fact that they are *her* letters by attributing them to another woman, indeed, another "other woman." In this way, Munro's device of the three-way split subject allows the narrator to approach her innermost self, the very expression of her symptom of jouissance, the way in which her desire speaks itself to the other, in love, the way her love writes itself. Moreover, in spite of her subsequent denial – "not mine," "not written by me" – she *knows* that they are her letters: "I knew I would find my letters." Following the map and reading the directory has led her to Barbara (a signifier, that of the barred Other at the limit of the symbolic), and taking hold of the bag of letters gives her access to Patricia, who signs them: from a signifier (Patricia means "noble") that names a subject, she is reduced to a common noun / verb "Pat" (to tap, to strike lightly), and then to P., a letter in the unconscious, a primordial, abject (Pee) trace of jouissance. As the necessary condition of non-self-recognition is fulfilled, she reads her P-letters.

In distorted form, the letters repeat the hopes and dreams of the narrator, going back to when she first felt that lovely sense of falling in love, back when her daughter was still in a stroller; this is written into the first letter as the memory of a time / place shared that held the promise of forever: "*My dear love, You leave me so happy. I went to the park with Samantha and it was lovely. I pushed her on the swings and watched her on the slide and thought I will have to love this park forever and ever, because I went there when I was so happy and after I had been with you*" (121). This letter (like those that follow) includes, beyond what is said intentionally (I'm happy when I think of you), smatterings of anxiety. Thus, the dream of "*forever and ever*" is undermined by the ambiguity of the very first sentence: "*You leave me so happy,*" where the strangeness of the verb "leave" (instead of the more usual "make") dominates and undermines the promise of happiness.

The second letter encodes disorientation and guilty panic through an anecdote about someone, a man, greedily eating fruit that was not meant to be eaten – "*they must be the ornamental plums, they are hard as rocks and nobody ever was meant to eat them I'm sure but I saw him grabbing them and swallowing them down by the handful*" (121). The letter is broken off in mid-sentence after mentioning "the purple cushions" – possibly a displaced form of the forbidden plums – that the couple had shared.

The third tells her lover of a dream: "You were holding my hair in your hands and saying, this is all too heavy for you, you'll have to cut it off, it will sap your strength. And the way you said it was so lovely, so sympathetic, as if you meant something else not just my hair. How can I tell, love, what you're saying in my dreams if you never write to me. So please write and tell me, tell me what you're saying to me in my dreams – " (121). Hair, a symbol of feminine sexuality, is judged by the lover to be excessive, surplus, and unnecessary. Often associated with loss of strength, the suggestion of cutting her hair implies the castration of the very Otherness in her that belongs to her as a desiring woman. In putting herself "in [his] hands," there is the risk that he might not recognize and value that Otherness that is constitutive of her position as a woman. This is her anxiety, but not her certainty – the meaning of his words, and his desire, remains obscure, remains a question.

The fourth letter spells out the central question in the story, and the justification for the death fantasy itself: "I could deal with my feelings if I had to and recover from loving you but I must know whether you love me and want me any more so please, please, tell me yes or no" (122). The insistence of the letter (the number of letters but also the insistent tone in the final one) expresses her desire to be relieved of the uncertainty that plagues her: she wants to know what the man wants. Yes or No. A simple answer. Since the answer never comes, definitively, fantasy precautions are taken: if the answer were to be No, how would she survive the "end of the world" feeling that Freud associates with the withdrawal of love from the subject's world: "The end of the world is the projection of this internal catastrophe" … "the withdrawal of love" from one's subjective universe ("Psychoanalytic Notes" 208–9).

At the same time, the insistence of the letter is apparent in that it replays the whole of the narrator's own history of love: falling in love, enjoying it, growing anxious about it, and confronting loss. Thus, the fantasy addresses not only the question of the other's desire, but also her own. How does she "see herself" when she confronts this version of herself in the letters of P.? An answer can be inferred from the narrator's choice of going to the place where the m(Other) holds her letters, and in her reaction to her "reading" of them: she can "recover from loving [him]" by "recover"ing the letter of her desire, by bringing her jouissance home, so as to desire again, and this implies "disposing" of her letters, in both senses of the word. Let's look at this a bit more closely.

Accepting that the narrator is the fundamental addressee of her own love letters allows us to understand Lacan's reference to the love letter as a sort of wall (*la lettre d'(a)mur*) on which one writes *oneself*: "So Lacan is speaking about love – and when you speak in the loving discourse, the discourse of love, you are speaking of yourself … You believe that you are speaking to the Other and speaking about the Other, but … you are speaking about yourself" (Soler, "Some Remarks"). Were the letters ever addressed to him? The bag is "full of letters," letters that never reached him, and since, for Lacan, the letter always arrives at its destination, it is in their return, first to the narrator, from Barbara, but more significantly – and here we recall the shopwoman's injunction, "whole damn lot's got to be returned" – *to* Barbara, as her exotic extimate double; it is only then that the letter arrives. How so? By reading her own letters, given back to her by Barbara, letters in which she encounters herself as P., the protagonist receives her message back from the Other in a distorted-dreamlike form, and she knows then what she has, in fact, always known – that there is a point beyond which she will not go:[21] the "last letter, really no letter at all, a large scribble on the page, without salutation or signature: *Please write to me or phone me, I am going crazy. I hate to be like this but it is more than I can stand so I beg you*" (122) reveals this point. The breakdown of her subjectivity, now without a signature, reduced to a scribble, a trace, a barely-letter-like thing, is the place of the real that she has glimpsed and from which she must either return or go "crazy."

Understood in terms of the real, affirms Žižek, the arrival of the letter is equivalent to "meeting one's fate" (*Enjoy* 25), or in other words, death. A disengagement from this place of her death (through his) begins – a process of the narrator's mourning the lost loving self she was in loving him. She returns the letters that she has held and read, to Barbara: "I've had a grief lately," she says to this guardian of her feminine opacity, to whom she "no longer want[s] to talk," then proceeds to distance herself from Patricia / P., the murky despairing libidinal trace of herself, who will either "figure it out" or "just have to … suffer" (123) and affirms that she herself is "going away." There is just one thing left to do with these love letters that "keep coming" with "no return address," and Barbara does it: "She holds the bag of letters over the wastebasket, lets it drop: 'I can't keep them around any more.' 'No,'" agrees the narrator (123). Indeed there is no need to: "what is repeated insists so much in order to get itself noticed" (Lacan, "Seminar on the Purloined Letter" 32), and that has been accomplished. The letter returns to litter, nonsignifying "signifiers" in the real,[22] unlinked to the signifying chain, outside of the symbolic circuit of exchange and desire. Since the "closing of the letter's circuit equals its consumption" (Žižek, *Enjoy* 25), it is now a dead letter. The image of *herself, in love*, has dissolved; and she is still there, intact, able to "go out into the street … and walk and walk" (124).

AFTER LOVE, LOVE, *ENCORE*

As if now situated on the other side of love, she looks back at it, at the worst of it, the suffering of "that girl Patricia. Girl, woman …" (124) and imagines her in her pain: "She sits in the dark … She walks around the rooms. She tries smiling at herself in the glass … She suffers according to rules we all know, which are meaningless and absolute. When I think of her I see all this sort of love as you must have seen, or see it, as something going on at a distance; a strange, not even pitiable, expenditure; unintelligible ceremony in an unknown faith" (124). A reversal of perspectives is attempted here, as if the return of the letters to litter has placed her beyond the wall of imaginary projections produced by love, and she can see clearly how strange the whole suffering business of love can appear, once outside of it. In counterpoint to the narrator's earlier characterization of men's chivalry and "obedience to secret orders" (116), the "faith" of women is "unintelligible" even to themselves, belonging to what is most opaque in subjective existence: suffering that is "meaningless and absolute," like the inescapable repetition of the symptom. If a woman is a man's symptom,[23] is love a woman's symptom?

It would seem that women cannot give up on love. No sooner has the narrator stepped out of her fantasy of the survival of its loss than she resumes her conversation with her lover: the quotation above is addressed to him – "as you must have seen, or see it," she says, rewriting him into the present tense. If the fantasy has offered some assurance that love's losses will not annihilate her, it has not put an end to her fundamental questioning of the man's desire. She persists, "Am I right, am I getting close to you, is that true?" (124). She might add: Tell me yes or no.

The end of the story therefore picks up on and continues the conversation whose structure of questioning might read as follows: If I, a woman, choose to love you (for it is a question of choice) or rather, having chosen to love you, can I trust you with my love? How can I frame this excess in me – the excess of my lack – that I have offered to you and that you treat lightly, answering or not answering as you will, giving or not giving an echo to my words of love? How can I protect myself from the ravages of your indifference, or my fear of your indifference, or the possibility that you might not recognize this gift of love? How can I know if my love satisfies you? My darling, can't you see, this uncertainty is killing me; to save myself, I must make you (my love) into a dead thing, I must kill you off so that my lack will come back to me and I can desire to love again. And now, will you, knowing that I could survive our love, trust me not to "flood" you with my love, and will you love me too?

This is the risk she cannot help but take, since love is the symptomatic path of her being. She does not, however, risk everything. She gives her love to him, she loves him, but not all of her love goes there. Even as she suffers from the tarrying of her liquid love into a parched landscape, she finds, in words, letters, and books, the wellspring of another love – the love of the letter. The books in Barbara's bookstore – in the den of the opaque place of jouissance – speak of happiness: "These books seem to me all the same – the happiness-and-peace ones and the magic wonders – they don't seem like separate books at all, that is why I cannot touch them. They are all flowing together around the store like some varicolored marvelous stream, or wide river, and I can really no more understand what is inside them than I can breathe underwater" (119). How very much like the streaming together of the lights of cars that announced the first glimmerings of love on the highway. Where there, she felt "urged to float upon the present," here too, she does not enter the river of books, does not "touch them," but "stare[s] at them in stupefaction": they are books, but they do not tell her anything specific. It is their testimony to faith in the possibility of happiness that creates the "oceanic" feeling and the conditions of possibility for the emergence of a singular love.[24]

After consenting to the disposal of P.'s letters, the final significant gesture of the narrator is to metaphorically crumple up her own consciously assumed letter – the story itself: "Never mind. I invented her. I invented you, as far as my purposes go. I invented loving you and I invented your death" (124). Thus, the content of the story and the lives that peopled it are swept aside, as if it could be disposed of so easily, as if by proclaiming four times "I invented" the whole story, its truth effects could be discounted or taken back. Yet, invention is not without truth: Lacan makes a rather bold statement to this effect – "I don't discover the truth, I invent it. And that, I might add, is what constitutes knowledge" (*SXXI,* 19 February 1974). This is incomprehensible from the point of view of what Lacan calls the master's discourse, that is, the discourse that presupposes that truth precedes knowledge and that science can "discover" it; that the world, including the world of subjectivity, is, *in theory,* "fully knowable." Rather, speaking from the reverse perspective – that of the analyst's discourse – truth refers to unconscious knowledge (*le savoir insu*) and arises from a subjective symptom that is libidinally fixed in a particular path of jouissance, and as such, in its subjective singularity, is always an invention.[25]

Moreover, invention is what likens the symptom to the literary work: "literary creation can be [understood as] a symptom because a symptom is itself an invention. What does it mean to create? The answer is: to bring something into being where there was nothing before. But saying 'where there was nothing,' I already imply a place. And there is no such thing as a place without the symbolic and its marks, and every symbolic mark engenders as empty the place it creates" (Soler, "Literature" 215). The invention of a story, a story about love, is a creation that marks as empty the place that it has come to fill. Love aims at this filling of a space: a place created as empty-to-be-filled by love, by the discourses, forms, myths, hopes, desires, and plans of love, and also by love's jouissance – "To speak of love is in itself a *jouissance*" (Lacan, *SXX* 83) – and the unconscious truth it bears.

Who, in "Tell Me Yes or No," engendered this space by making love appear, by bringing it into existence there where it was not? There is an almost childlike accusing tone in the narrator's complaint: "But you were the one, I keep forgetting, *you were the one who said it first*" (124): the one who said "I love you." Is this a plea for her lover to accept authorship, to accept responsibility, to acknowledge what it shifted in her universe to be invited to invent love in this space he opened up through speech? While the context (the end of the fantasy of the lover's death) leads the reader to hear the phrase in the tone of blame, is there not also a form of reiteration of the hysteric's question, formulated as an injunction that he "answer her!"? In response to the hysteric's plea, "speech is demanded, nothing else. The one who acknowledges this injunction, or mandate to speak, is given the power to satisfy the Demand. This constitutes him as the capital Other. By posing the riddle, the hysteric commands the Other from her position as agent, and yet in so doing entirely surrenders to him whom she empowers to answer: 'Tell me! Answer me! Whatever you say I am!'" (Wajcman). The narrator's demand is indeed rephrased immediately afterwards as a question, one that expands outward from herself to include a chorus of women: the Emily R.s and Martha T.s of the magazine's case histories (117), asking the question, "How are we to understand you?" (124). We women, you men, caught up in the web of each other's desire.

Love is not the resolution to the sexual relation that does not exist; that is, it does not do away with the disharmony of the desires and jouissances of the sexes, nor that of the singularity of the two who try to come together in love. It is this persistent wish to efface the distance between the lover and the beloved that makes of love an impossible (if necessary) dream: "Love is impotent, though mutual, because it is not aware that it is but the desire to be One, which leads us to the impossibility of establishing the relationship between 'them-two' (*la relation d'eux*). The relationship between them-two what? – them-two sexes" (Lacan, *SXX* 6). In other words, it is because we desire the return to an imaginary state of nonlack, which is impossible, and because love, desire, and sexual jouissance give fantasmatic shape to this wish but cannot fulfill it, that there is no relationship (in the sense of logical correspondence or natural complementarity) between the sexes: they always miss each other to some degree. Lack is constitutive of subjectivity; neither sex makes up for what is missing in the other: nothing can, nothing does, except death, where nothing is missing. Love is the scene where the impossibility of the sexual relationship is played out, over and over, *encore* et *en-corps*. On this stage, the narrator is fully present in love – "Undeniably. Yes." (113) – but also retains within herself a slight distance from herself and her love, a space of self-preservation: "I have my tricks and my trap doors, too. I don't understand their workings at the present moment, but I have to be careful, I won't speak against them" (124). The lovely, uncertain tricks of invention and storytelling to shore oneself up against the risks and misfortunes of love.

LOVE'S (UN)ENDINGS

The "end" of the relationship is not given, the "answer" to the narrator's question never arrives, the persistency of the question being the only answer possible. Munro's later stories continue the refrain of questioning love: I've already mentioned "Simon's Luck" (1978), which deals with the uncertainty of love through the woman's choice to "run away" from it, fearing love's risks more than she believes in its promises; that story's conclusion, which reveals that Simon's failure to keep their date was due to an illness from which he will die, implies that had she trusted a bit further, a short space and time of love might have been possible. In a story called "Accident" from Munro's next collection, *The Moons of Jupiter* (1982), the passion of the beginnings of love is intertwined with the complications and complexities of a long-term relationship. The man loved by the central female figure is, in succession, married, a grieving father, no longer married, her husband, and finally, her late husband. As the narration looks back with the protagonist over her life, she notes that "She's had her love, her scandal, her man, her children. But inside she's ticking away, all by herself, the same Frances who was there before any of it" (109). Love is central, shapes a lifetime, and yet does not efface the indelible letter of the individual's subjectivity, in spite of all the vagaries of the "accidents" of life, love, and passion.

Before leaving the Munrovian field of love, I will mention one last image of a possible ending to the story of love. In "What Do You Want to Know For?" (*View*), published in 2006, the landscape figures differently; no longer the metaphorical support for a broken heart, it is the very setting in which the story unfolds as the narrator travels along in these late stories, which Munro qualified as "closer to my own life than the other stories I had written, even in the first person" ("Foreword," *View* xii). In a car with her husband, looking for a particular road, she notes: "it was a pleasure, as always, to be together in this part of the world looking at the countryside that we think we know so well and that is always springing some sort of surprise on us" (318). The quiet reference to "a pleasure, as always, to be together," abandons the spectacular or dramatic in favour of a simple pleasure renewed.

Is this a later scene from the love story that began on the highway under the fiery pink sky in the 1970s? Is it a streaming together of all the loves, and hopes of love, of all the women narrators of the Munrovian universe, including the multiple selves each one is to herself? Consulting the geological map, "reading" the landscape through the car window, she notes: "[T]here is always more than just the keen pleasure of identification. There's the fact of these separate domains, each with its own history and reason, its favorite crops and trees and weeds … each with its special expression, its pull on the imagination. The fact of these little countries lying snug and unsuspected" (322). As a site of subjective projection, the landscape takes on the value of an infinite field of exploration – that of the "snug and unsuspected" countries of the self, encountered here in a scene of shared pleasure. We leave our questioning on this image of a land prone to "springing … surprises," even on those who "know [it] well," the land of the ceaseless discovery of the other, in love.

III

Epilogue

The Truth of the Fixion

The road taken in my analyses of Alice Munro's stories has led from what is most graspable in fiction – the structures of meaning – to the point where meaning stops. This is true both in terms of the progression from the stories of early childhood to the stories of adult relationships and sexuality, and in terms of the advancement of the analytic commentaries per se. In the analysis of the childhood stories, my reading has tended toward a resituating of the latent content of the stories within recognizable structures of meaning – the fairy tale family romance fantasy in "Royal Beatings," or the deciphering of the return of the repressed as symptomatic of an obscure trauma in "Princess Ida." With "Boys and Girls," the story resists any gesture of tidy reconfiguring, notably of the question of sexual identity, and confronts the reader instead with the emergence of the real in the subjective act – an unforeseen moment in which meaning, the body, and the unconscious path of desire find themselves aligned in a direction that runs opposite to the symbolic law and that grounds a new direction of subjectivity; the necessity of the open gate imposes itself on the girl in such a way that all of her being is engaged in its affirmation.

The stories of the second group, in which the protagonist is an adult woman, have, of necessity, led me toward the laying bare of a more complex knot of subjectivity since the question of sexual difference, and notably of the nonrelationship of the jouissances of men and women, is the very stuff of the narratives. In each case, but each time differently, the narrative offers a perspective on the ways in which the disharmony of the sexes is played out: how the set of the all-phallic, closed, masculine universal founded on the exception, and the not-all phallic, open, feminine nonuniversal, repeatedly miss each other. And also, how people suffer because of it: because of the impossibility at the heart of the dream of concordance between the two. The suffering reveals what lacks, or what is desired, for the women in the Munrovian universe: what is desired is to be loved in a way that leaves no room for doubt. Thus, they suffer. But what is revealed to each through their pain is of the order of a "symptomatic singularity" (Soler, *Lacan* ch. 10): for Mary Jo in "Eskimo," it is a glimpse of a knowledge related to her structuring sexual fantasy and, beyond that, to the place of attachment to the maternal Thing; for Sophia in "Too Much Happiness," it is the experience of a jouissance that cannot be captured in words and that overflows the possibility of conceptualization and bears witness to an intensity of being even as she is about to die. In "Tell Me Yes or No," the very inscrutability of the otherness of the other, and the other as man, torments the woman in her loving dependence on him.

All of the stories, in their various developments, contain a baffling image or a knot of perplexity around which the narrative *marks* its sublimating path and organizes its unfolding: the beating in "Royal Beatings"; the dark core of the mother's past in "Princess Ida"; the sight of the father killing the horse in "Boys and Girls." In "Eskimo" the images are multiple: the woman licking the face of her partner, the broken doll on the bathroom floor, and the blue "court" flowers in the mysterious sari-wrapped woman's hand. And in "Tell Me Yes or No," the empty letter box. In "Too Much Happiness," the baffling core is there as the mysterious illness to be avoided at all costs and that presents to the woman, who is already "sick," an unsolvable riddle. This impenetrable mystery is that of mortality itself, and the impossibility of going beyond it produces the tension that culminates in Sophia's ecstatic last words.

It also produces, in the work of Munro, the necessity of starting again, of trying over and over again to revitalize and clarify the inscrutable stain of jouissance around which the narratives of lives revolve. Munro writes about this continually renewed process in her "Introduction" to *The Moons of Jupiter*, using an image that brings the written story into the Lacanian field of the objet a: "The story is a kind of extension of myself, something once attached to me and growing out of me, now lopped off, exposed and abandoned. What I feel isn't shame or regret exactly – it would be quite hypocritical to say I felt that, when exposure, publication was surely what I had in mind all along – rather it's a queasiness, an unwillingness to look or examine. I try to master this, feeling that it's primitive and childish" (xiii). There are echoes here of the Lacanian myth of the lamella, at the very place where Munro writes about her relationship to her stories.

The lamella names the Lacanian myth of origins, a *myth* of pure libido based on the cast off, abandoned, fetal membrane from which the newborn baby emerges: "[The lamella] is the libido, *qua* pure life instinct, that is to say, immortal life, or irrepressible life, life that has need of no organ, simplified, indestructible life. It is precisely what is subtracted from the living being by virtue of the fact that it is subject to the cycle of sexed reproduction. And it is of this that all the forms of the *objet a* that can be enumerated are the representatives, its figures" (Lacan, *SXI* 198). Existing, like the objet a, in an "ectopic rather than an internal relation to the subject" (Barnard, "Tongues" 180), Munro sees her stories as "once attached" but now "lopped off" from her. The lost object, as lamella, is both lost and ever present; as libido it remains *intimately external* to the subject in the real, creating effects: for Munro they are effects of exposure, of "shame," "queasiness," "an unwillingness to look."

The unwillingness to look participates in a form of forgetting so that she remarks: "I have to make an effort, now, to remember what's in these stories. That's a strange thing. I make them with such energy and devotion and secret pains, and then I wiggle out and leave them, to harden and settle in their place. I feel free" ("Introduction" xv). This is a remarkable account of the process of artistic sublimation whereby the author shapes her art with "energy," "devotion," and "pain," inhabiting the object libidinally, and then leaves the artefact as a sloughed skin or membrane, something one can wiggle out of. But in spite of its finished appearance as "hardened and settled," the lamella that inhabits the specific objects of the drive is "indestructible" precisely because "the lamella does not exist, it *insists.*" It is the way in which Lacan rewrites the Freudian death drive, making it, paradoxically, into "its very opposite" (Žižek, *How to Read* 62); that is to say, the death drive is seen in this perspective as homologous with the libido, which emerges from the place of nothingness, and without which drive, desire, and love would be unthinkable.

Hence, the lamella, the abandoned self, the unwanted remainder / reminder of the past insists, in a way that is particular to each individual, and pushes her toward repetition: "Next thing I know I've started assembling the makings; I'm getting ready to do the whole thing over again" (Munro, "Introduction," *The Moons of Jupiter* xv–xvi). There is no stopping point for the libidinal force of the drive, which does not achieve satisfaction in attaining an end point or a teleological goal (which will always come up short) but in the very process of circling round, and thereby bringing into being, its objects (Copjec, *Imagine* 38).

The process of sublimation, which is this devotedness to the object of the drive, provides satisfaction. For each person, the path is singular, and originates in the specificity of his or her lalangue, the fertile bed of signifiers unsignified, of letters inherited as a potentiality of being. In this alluvial deposit, left by the "water of language" (Soler, *Lacan* ch. 3), are to be found the nuggets of jouissance. Ranging from the word to the sentence, to larger structures of discourse, language is *joui:* enjoyed. The speaking being gets off, for better or worse, on language, on the echo in the body of its effects, on the sparks, tickles, weightiness, lusty inventiveness, and transformative power of language; on the joy, pain, release, satisfaction, predictability, and unending renewal of its possibilities.

My perspective throughout the analyses has been to avoid psychobiography, but it is clear from what I have just said that the singular path of jouissance, as it can be read in the writing of an author, has something to do with the person who writes, the individual whose consistency of "saying" gives us a sense of the thematic and stylistic coherence of their work. In Soler's view of Lacan's theorectical elaborations, the debate about the early versus the later or even final Lacan imposes a form of chronology that "elides the One that links all the textual variations. This One is not at the level of theses but at the level of what I call the choice that grounds a unique saying (un dire unique), beyond the variations of statements (les dits)" (*Lacan* ch. 1).[1] What is the "unique saying" of Munro – her signature, or "signerature"[2] – etched in the specificity of her subjective position at a specific historico-cultural-libidinal nexus, in the traces of her writing?

The catalogue (an incongruous idea) of the pleasures and specificities of Alice Munro's writing would be infinite: there is no "all" to be established here, and there is clearly variation of linguistic and structural emphasis in her stories. The abundant use of simile in her early stories, and the more complex layering of her later stories, attest to this. Simply, there are forms of repetition throughout her work that might usefully be considered as bearing witness to the path of singularity her work follows and that belong to, but do not exhaust the meaning of, her ways of doing things with words. I would like to consider a few examples of marks of the Munrovian style, those that are indexes of a symptomatic "saying" and that constitute the signature of her fiction or *fixion*, to use Lacan's neologism, which condenses "fiction" and "fixation." Some of these markers are, as I see it, the reworking of narrative lines, the persistence of the affect of humiliation, and, more idiosyncratically, the omnipresence of references to "linoleum."

Examples of reworked stories are numerous: this struck me with force on reading "The Progress of Love" (*Progress*), a variant of the story "Princess Ida." I have posited that the emotional structure of "Princess Ida" concerns a daughter focusing on her mother and on the mother's pain, a hurt that reaches back to that mother's relation to her own mother and is somehow related to the debasement of an ideal of sexuality due to a male family member, her brother. All of this constitutes a family *unsaid*, a silence encircling a wound that will divide the siblings concerning their view of the past, and that will prompt questioning on the part of the daughter. "The Progress of Love" rewrites this story from a different slant. The following chart allows us to see the shifts in the distribution of subjective positions:

"Princess Ida"	"The Progress of Love"
Del (narrating voice)	Fame (narrating voice)
• Del's mother (Addie, injured party)	• Fame's mother (Marietta, religious)
• Bill (Addie's hated sibling, now American) + Nile (his wife)	• Beryl (Marietta's sibling, now American)
• Del's grandmother (religious)	• Fame's grandmother (injured party) and grandfather (hated father of Marietta)

In "The Progress of Love," narrated by a woman named Fame, the figures of Del's mother and grandmother become condensed into that of Marietta, Fame's mother, seen praying "on her knees at midday, at night, and first thing in the morning" (4). This leaves space for a different construction of the maternal grandmother, the woman who will be "tortured" in a "barn" (exchanging places here with Del's own mother): the "torture" will be a near- or pretend-hanging suicide, and therefore not directly inflicted by a male figure, except that this near-suicide attempt is a response to her husband's sexual infidelity with "some girl that kept coming round to the works" (28). Fame's mother, Marietta, a witness to her own mother's threatened hanging, takes on the burden of her mother, whose "heart was broken" (17), through her hatred of her father.

As a child, Fame does not understand Marietta's hatred of her own father, but prods at it through her questioning. About her mother's hair gone white, Fame asks: "'Weren't you sad when it went white?' 'No. I was glad.' 'Why?' 'I was glad that I wouldn't have hair anymore that was the same color as my father's'" (8). The answer here is far more direct than the mother's circumvolutions in "Princess Ida": antipathy is affirmed.

When it comes time for the visit that will allow for a confrontation with the past, in the place of Del's mother and Uncle Bill, who are directly concerned by the conflict in "Princess Ida," a surrogate victim and a surrogate victimizer are present: Marietta and Beryl. Beryl is interesting in that she is a condensed version of both Bill and Nile from "Princess Ida." Like Bill, she has become an American, she was present in the barn watching the mother standing on a chair with a rope around her neck, and she is associated with mishandling a cat, holding it "up by the front legs" (17). Like Nile, that green nail-polished exemplar of feminine fashion, Beryl is first seen as "so glamorously got up that it was hard to tell whether she was good-looking, or happy, or anything" (20), but gone grotesque: Beryl is revealed, having washed her face, to have skin that "was pale now, covered with fine cracks, rather like the shiny mud at the bottom of puddles drying up in early summer" (22). Like Bill, buying up the local store, she will use her money to "buy" the family, taking them out to dinner, and then will start revising the past, defending the father and casting the scorned mother in the role of the one who "went too far" (29). The two sisters, Beryl and Marietta, are therefore lined up in terms of sides to be taken: the mother's hurt to be defended versus the de-dramatizing of the father's infidelity.

This conflict comes to a head over the inheritance left to each of the girls by the father: for Beryl, it is a legitimate inheritance and can be accepted. For Marietta, the three thousand dollars (ten times the money Del's mother is to receive) is poisoned money, associated with the father's fault and the mother's broken heart, and cannot be accepted. More radical than Del's mother, who deals with hurt through irony, Marietta burns the money. Fame, recounting this to a lover / friend, names the mother's feeling: "she burned it up because she hated him. She didn't want his money. She hated him" (35).

Whereas in "Princess Ida" the mother's feeling of hurt announces the close of the story, in "The Progress of Love" there is a further, final shift. Fame has written something new into her memory of the past: the presence of her father watching her mother burn the money, "letting her do it" (35), understanding her need or right to accomplish that gesture. "I consider that love," says Fame (35). When it then turns out that her memory is untrue, that the father was not present, it does not alter her verdict: the scene may not be "true," but the love that produced the imperfect memory was. Strangely, the need to comfort the mother in "Princess Ida" has been reworked through "The Progress of Love" as a need to reinstate the father figure, to make a space for fathers, for men. Her friend, Bob Marks, tells Fame, "You don't need to be so tough on us" (40), and Fame would seem to agree, musing that "moments of kindness and reconciliation are worth having, even if the parting has to come sooner or later" (41). This has less poetic and emotional density than "the downflash of a wing or knife," but seems to bear witness to a revised subjective distance on the mother figure: the narrator, at the end of "The Progress of Love," is reaching toward a way of moving out from under that "cloud you couldn't see through or get to the end of" associated, in Fame's view, with the mother, a cloud that she, when she would upset her mother, "became a part of" to such an extent that she felt burdened with "a really sickening shame" (17). Unable to evince the inexplicable sense of shame, the narrator, in focusing on the father's position as the bearer of love for his wife, seems to be shaping an alternate form of compensation for her mother's hurt.

Narrative reworkings of this sort are numerous in Munro's stories, as are more limited refashionings of specific scenes or emotional, affective configurations. The predominant one in Munro's work is the joint experience of shame and humiliation.[3] In Munro's earlier writings, shame is, unsurprisingly, a negative experience, but humiliation is often associated with a certain paradoxical jouissance; in "Sunday Afternoon" (*Dance*), we read the musings of a girl who has ended a stretch of work as a maid in a well-to-do family's summer retreat, and who is kissed, out of the blue, by a relative of the family she works for: "This stranger's touch had eased her; her body was simply grateful and expectant, and she felt a lightness and confidence she had not known in this house. So there were things she had not taken into account, about herself … But things always came together; there was something she would not explore yet – a tender spot, a new and still mysterious humiliation" (170–1). Humiliation, here, is the counterpoint to another feeling, that of "lightness and confidence," but it is not connoted as entirely negative: "tender," "new," and "mysterious" clear open a positive space around it.

In "Heirs of the Living Body" (*Lives*), Del experiences humiliation when tickled by her cousin, Mary-Agnes Oliphant, an occasion that reminds her of another, "exquisite" humiliation: "Having to be naked myself, the thought of being naked, stabbed me with shame in the pit of my stomach. Every time I thought of the doctor pulling down my pants and jabbing the needle in my buttocks, for smallpox, I felt outraged, frantic, unbearably, almost exquisitely, humiliated" (49). The word "exquisitely," coming on the heels of such a slew of negative adjectives, captures the paradoxical nature of jouissance, its at-the-limitness where pain and pleasure are not clearly distinguishable. In this case, as above, humiliation is associated with the idea that something unknown about oneself is being revealed: "I was amazed as people must be who are seized and kidnapped, and who realize that in the strange world of their captors they have a value absolutely unconnected with anything they know about themselves" (48). Indeed, as suggested in the previous chapter, on "Tell Me Yes or No," this extimate place of opacity is the place of being itself.

In my analysis of "Royal Beatings," I explored not only the beating received by Rose in the story, but also its relationship to another version of the same episode in the memoir-story called "Fathers" (*View*).

In the first, humiliation dominates the emotional field, whereas in the second, shame is prevalent. Indeed, in "Fathers," in the narrator's comment on her feeling of "Perpetual shame. Exposure" (195), the temporal marker "perpetual" situates the event at the existential level of subjective being, as the experience of being seen in one's mortal finitude and bodily vulnerability. Lacan linked the experience of shame to existential being when he merged the French word for shame, *honte*, with "ontology" to produce "*hontology*, to finally give it its correct spelling" (*SXVII*, 17 June 1970). Where the more freely fictional "Royal Beatings" conveyed a certain jouissance of humiliation, the "closer-to-my-own-life" writing of "Fathers" emphasizes shame, and notably, in the eyes of the father.

This eye of the father has been lurking in the margins of some of the stories I have considered: in the mirror for the girl in "Boys and Girls" as a conjoined image of the ego-Ideal and the obscene father marking the place of death, and in the linoleum that "leer[s] up" at Rose in "Royal Beatings." In fact, even in "Boys and Girls," linoleum is associated with an ambiguous male presence, as both soldier and criminal: in the children's bedroom was "a soldiery roll of linoleum, standing on end" and "whenever a man escaped from the county jail, [the girl] imagined that he had somehow let himself in the window and was hiding behind the linoleum" (112–13). The prevalence of references to linoleum in Munro's stories is indeed quite striking. As a typical, economic floor covering of the period of Munro's childhood, its presence might seem unextraordinary. Yet the fact that it is commonplace, hardly noteworthy, gives it an uncanny effect when it suddenly surges into a scene.

The word *linoleum*, with its extravagant Latin form, is often reduced to "lino" in popular usage, but never so in Munro's writing: the word always remains in the full form of its incongruous signifier, four syllables long and yet fluid in its opening / closing vowel and consonant alterations. From common noun, it takes on the status as the proper name of the gaze: the place from which the self is seen in its secret, mortal, sexual, shameful being. Occasionally it lies quietly under dancing feet, barely suggesting the disorder of sentiments in the room: "Round and round the linoleum, me proud, intent, Nora laughing and moving with great buoyancy, wrapping me in her strange gaiety, her smell of whisky, cologne, and sweat" ("Walker Brothers Cowboy,"

Dance 16); at times it functions with more insistence to signal an oncoming disaster, in this case, a child's death: "She kicked at a crust of porridge that had dried on the linoleum. Lookit that, she said. Lookit *that*! What's it always a mess around here for?" ("The Time of Death," *Dance* 94);[4] or it may mark an absence, associated with the as-yet unconscious knowledge of death: "Her footprints showed on the carpet and on the linoleum tiles, and outside on the snow" ("Fits," *Progress* 161).

Elsewhere, the surface lends its support to metaphors of obscure illumination: "The moonlight came through the kitchen window – she was sitting in the dark – and she watched a patch of light shift through the night, on the linoleum, and disappear" ("The Love of a Good Woman," *The Love of* 71); of the disarrangement of life: "I remember the floor of the living room, which was covered with left-over squares and rectangles of linoleum – all the different colors and patterns fitted together and stitched like a crazy quilt" ("Cortes Island," *The Love of* 140); or of the place of original passionate attachment: "She cried because she and Polly had laughed as they cleaned the kitchen shelves and scrubbed the linoleum the day before, and she had pretended she was in a sentimental play and said good-bye, old linoleum, good-bye, crack in the teapot, good-bye, the place where I used to stick my gum under the table, good-bye" ("Post and Beam," *Hateship, Friendship* 196).

In "Post and Beam," linoleum marks the presence / absence, not of family, but of desire's object. In a room visited by the narrator, and in the absence of the young man who lives there and who stirs vague sentiments in her, she observes: "A Venetian blind stuck halfway down the window, and a square of linoleum whose pattern was covered by brown paint" (202). The absence of verbal structure in the description creates a sense of shifting momentarily outside of time, where the linoleum square takes on the aspect of that stain in the painting that niggles at one's perception of the whole, pulling the gaze toward an obscure vortex. Covered in unglamorous brown paint, the square of linoleum here suggests both ordinariness and concealment: secrets to be revealed. But there are none: the opacity is, in itself, the mystery. The square finally takes on the function of situating and focusing a sort of unspecified desirousness on the part of the woman: "What she really wanted to do was not to investigate anymore but to sit down on the floor, in the middle of the square of linoleum. To sit for hours not so much looking at this room as sinking into it. To stay in this room where there was nobody who knew her or wanted a thing from her. To stay here for a long, long time, growing sharper and lighter, light as a needle" (203). The square of linoleum in this scene is suggestive of the opaque place of jouissance from which desire emerges as cause, as desire-for-something, or as desirousness before it takes on its aims or symptom-objects (Soler, *Lacan* ch. 15). In this sense, the desire to sink into an undefined time-space and be transformed, pared down, freed up, to become sharp and bright again suggests an encounter with desire as desire for something else: "Lacan enumerated some of the forms of indeterminate desire which dominate the desire for something else: boredom, prayer, watching, waiting" (Soler, *Lacan* ch. 15). What the story leads toward, however, is precisely the renouncement of giving this something else a specific form, and quite logically, this renunciation of taking on specific objects of desire translates into an impulse to pray: "So, nothing now but what she or anybody could sensibly foresee. That was to be her happiness, that was what she had bargained for. Nothing secret, or strange. Pay attention to this, she thought. She had a dramatic notion of getting down on her knees. This is serious" (218). The theatrical tone of the last lines, and the addendum to the ending of the short story – "It was a long time ago that this happened … When she was twenty-four years old, and new to bargaining" (218) – suggests that this, for all its subjective truth of the moment, is not the last word on the protagonist's desire, which, of course, remains open to the contingencies of life.

Linoleum, with its edges, patterns, possibilities of being covered over, repainted, in its newness or faded neglect, to be looked at or to be gazed at by, is a personal, malleable symbol, and there are certainly others in Munro's universe. Perhaps such personal symbols are a way of approaching the truth of our personal fixions that, on occasion, find their echo in the lalangue of others who respond with a sort of transferential love: how many of Munro's readers have felt that she has articulated *their* truths? Yet if it is true that "articulated truth is powerless to say the real that governs it" (Soler, *Lacan* ch. 2), then there is no "truth" in the sense of final meaning to be found in those unlikely

Munrovian "caves paved with kitchen linoleum," an incongruous mixing of metaphors that is doubtless so often quoted because of the rhyming force of "caves" and "paved" and the suggestion of hidden truths to be revealed; but "the truth never concludes …; it persists. We repress it and it returns; we gag it and it speaks elsewhere; we ask it to say the last word … and it only half-says" (Soler, *Lacan* ch. 2). Deciphering can take us so far, as far as language goes, but some of the truth remains inaccessible, inarticulably mired in the opacity of the real unconscious.

"What Do You Want to Know For?" This is the title of a story – the one that ends the section of close-to-the-self narratives in *The View from Castle Rock*, but it would equally be an appropriate subtitle for another story, "Dulse" (*The Moons*), where the narrator questions the value of self-knowledge. In an "analysis" scene, uncharacteristic of Munro's narratives, Lydia, the protagonist, is suffering from a broken heart. She replies to the doctor's question – "So, why are you with somebody who can always pull the rug out?" – with a volley of questions of her own: "Isn't there always somebody? When I was married it was me. Do you think it helps to ask these questions? Suppose it's just pride? I don't want to be alone, I want everybody to think I've got such a desirable man? Suppose it's the humiliation, I want to be humiliated? What good will it do me to know that?" (55). What good indeed is it to recognize one's essential dependency on the Other, to the extent that one's very self is put at stake, exposed and revealed as lacking? The doctor gives no reply, sending the question back to her: "I don't know. What do you think?" (55).

Embracing lack, in itself a "humiliation" for the ego, nevertheless allows one to make use of it, to identify with it as the cause of desire, to welcome it in desire's objects, which are, in Munro's narratives, love and lovers, but they are also, for the reader, the artistic sublimations that are the stories themselves. "Lopped off" and seemingly "hardened" into fixed form, says Munro, her narratives nonetheless go on, insinuating themselves into the lives of girls and women, shifting, morphing, insisting.

Notes

INTRODUCTION

Throughout this volume, where no translator is indicated in the bibliographical reference to a text originally in French, the translation is mine.

1 See Verhaeghe, "Lacan's Answer" 124.

2 The word is impossible to render fully in English: its French connotations include but are not reducible to enjoyment, legal entitlement, pleasure, orgasm, pain, thrill, ecstasy, or joy, none of which come anywhere near communicating the force of *jouissance,* which takes some of its intensity from its active verbal form – *jouir.*

3 The importance of the "letter" is also audible in the aforementioned neologism, *parlêtre,* which allows for equivocation with the phrase *par lettre* (by letter).

4 Having said that, the value of Lacan's writing is also this: to raise unthought-of questions.

5 One such example occurs in Margaret Atwood's *Surfacing,* where the protagonist uses an image close to Freud's, referring to a pearl, a "black pearl" (139) inside of her, to name the paradoxically sinister and yet precious (because symptomatically hers) embodiment of the negation of her own desire.

6 Lacanian critics point out that jouissance, per se, is unbearable: "I shall have to add that *jouissance* isn't very nice" (Adams 186); "Jouissance is simply overrated" (Fink, *A Clinical Introduction* 174).

7 A recently published article by Laura Dawkins also proposes a close reading of this scene from "Images." Her analysis relies upon the Freudian notion of the uncanny as the "familiar stranger within" to account for the

simultaneous shock and recognition experienced by the girl. Following the images in the text, Dawkins argues that the child, in perceiving the man in the woods, "fashions a homicidal stranger to *counter* her father's own latent aggression" (149, my emphasis). In my view, it would be closer to the point to say *account for* the father's potential for aggression. In other words, at this moment in the story, the man, Joe Phippen, gives form to the "father" who inhabits the register of the real – the eternal dead father, outside of generation and change: "All my life I had known there was a man like this and he was behind doors, just around the corner at the dark end of a hall" (Munro, "Images" 38). No man in particular, he threatens because, as perceived in the real, he escapes mortality and wields power over the insignificant "All my life" of the child.

Moreover, I would argue that he does not arise from the child's supposed "parricidal wish," as Dawkins suggests, but from the recognition that her father, both familiar and strange to her, includes this morbid dimension. His first words to Joe Phippen go in this direction: "Joe, you know me." The father, in his symbolic role of upholding the consistency of social bonds, speaks to Joe, who stands for that which cannot be encompassed by the register of the symbolic; he speaks calmly to rein in this "other": "I thought you'd recognize me, Joe." It is not surprising that the real does not recognize the symbolic in this moment of uncanny disturbance in the story.

Thus, where Dawkins sees the child's self-image in the moment of fear, where she is "like a child in an old *negative*, electrified against the dark noon sky" ("Images" 38, my emphasis) as that of "the child's darker self" (149), I would suggest that the image gives visual form to the emergence of the child's awareness of herself as potentially *negated*. The "wish," in other words, is not a wish for some particular thing – her father's death – but is the expression of a form of jouissance at the proximity of death; it is this morbid "kernel of enjoyment," to employ Žižek's term (*The Sublime Object* 74), that gives the experience the sense of emerging out of the "hope of something final, terrifying" ("Images" 38). Rather than trying to personalize the effects of the uncanny, it may be more useful to see it as the experience of a sense of the reassuring world suddenly being unhinged by the awareness of death, of one's own mortality. It is this awareness that is both denied and recognized in the fantasy formation.

8 The quotation within is from Lacan, *SVII* 76.

9 Translation slightly modified.

"ROYAL BEATINGS"

1 "The first thing to say about the unconscious … is what Freud says about it: it consists of thoughts" (Lacan, qtd in Fink, *A Clinical Introduction* 112).

2 *Lalangue* is generally rendered as llanguage in English translations (cf. Fink's translation of Lacan's *SXX* 44), but the impossibility of "hearing" the difference in pronunciation leads me prefer to keep the French *lalangue.* Rabaté's suggested translation, "lallalanguage" (*Jacques Lacan* 31), makes the sound difference audible, but its length makes it unwieldy.

3 It was later changed to *The Beggar Maid* for sale outside Canada, for copyright reasons.

4 "Everyone makes jokes about macaroni, because it is a hole with something around it, or about canons. The fact that we laugh doesn't change the situation, however: the fashioning of the signifier and the introduction of a gap or a hole in the real is identical" (Lacan, *SVII* 150).

5 The solemn temples, the great globe itself,
Ye all which it inherit, shall dissolve
And, like this insubstantial pageant faded,
Leave not a rack behind. We are such stuff
As dreams are made on, and our little life
Is rounded with a sleep. (Shakespeare, *The Tempest*, 4.1, 1883–9)

6 Sabrina Francesconi's recent article, "Alice Munro and the Poetics of the Linoleum," explores the polysemic usage of linoleum in Munro's work, and in particular, in the collection *Dance of the Happy Shades.*

7 See, for example, Janet Beer's "Short Fiction with Attitude."

8 Or rather, is lifted, by Brian, who remains outside of the conflict at hand, but who is convoked into its imagery. Note the use of the word "loosens" here, also used later to describe her father's face when the beating begins: "His face loosens and changes and grows younger" (18). The two masculine figures are thus metonymically associated.

9 "This is the way psychoanalysis subverts the usual opposition of the paternal and the maternal: it brings out what this opposition has to repress, to exclude, in order to establish itself, namely the *reverse* of the father, the 'anal father' who lurks behind the Name of the Father *qua* bearer of the symbolic Law … The mad 'anal father' is the nauseous debauchee, threatening yet ridiculously impotent" (Žižek, *Enjoy* 145–6).

10 The three phases are "My father is beating a child"; "I am being beaten by my father"; and "A child is being beaten." See Freud, "A Child Is Being Beaten."

11 See Murray and Garner on the question of theatricality in Munro's stories.

12 I have modified Alan Sheridan's translation: the phrase in French is *Veut-il me perdre?* Sheridan's translation "Can he lose me?" does not render the desiring aspect of the verb *vouloir*.

13 The short story "Fathers" (*The View)* offers an alternative version of the beating, as mentioned above, and it is also a similarly doubled or framed story, where the character of Becky Tyde finds a parallel in the childhood friend, named Dahlia, of the "Munro" persona. I have analyzed the difference in libidinal affect between the earlier and later stories in my article "Honte et Humiliation."

"PRINCESS IDA"

1 This statement from an interview in 1994 is coherent with Munro's earlier remarks (1983): "'Princess Ida' was the first. It was going to be a short story. Then I saw it was going to work into a novel, and then I went on and on writing what I thought was a novel. Then I saw that wasn't working. So I went back and picked out of that novel 'Princess Ida' in its original form" (Struthers 24–5).

2 The mother is referred to as Ada but once in "Princess Ida," pityingly, by the aunts: "Poor Ada" (73), and as Addie only by her brother, Bill. Del, hearing her uncle use this name, reflects: "No one ever called my mother Addie any more. It made her sound different – rounder, dowdier, simpler" (92). For Del, she is simply "my mother."

3 Earlier critics who *have* focused on this story have generally labelled Del's mother as "a pathetic and eccentric misfit" (MacDonald), or have blown her image somewhat out of proportion: "Like the Egyptian deity Isis … the mother is the essence of mysterious, powerful female first beginnings as well as a model of intellectual womanhood" (Rasporich 46).

4 "The Progress of Love" can, in fact, be shown to be a reconfiguring of "Princess Ida," with a similar emotional grievance passed down along the maternal line and with many of the structuring elements of this story present in condensed or displaced form in its later reworked version. I develop this idea in the epilogue to this work.

5 Indeed, the overarching perspective of the adult Del frames the story of her mother between two seasons of "going on the road" to sell encyclopedias (72, 101).

6 There is an interesting instance of disavowal in relation to this passage on the part of E.D. Blodgett, who affirms that "the only clue the reader has of [the brother] comes midway in a recollection of him as a cruel, fat boy who tortures cats, it is implied, in a sexual fashion" (45–6). The reference to sexuality has been noted, but its connection to Del's mother has been effaced through displacement onto the cat. This leaves Blodgett in the peculiar position of noting that this anecdote is "briefly sandwiched into the story of Del's grandmother's death and it appears to possess no particular function" (46).

7 In the story "Baptizing," which comes later in *Lives of Girls and Women*, Del's mother is portrayed in a manner that is reminiscent of the grandmother: when Del comes in after meeting her lover in the late evening, "there would be my mother sitting up in bed, the light shining right through her hair to her tender scalp, her cup of tea gone cold on the table beside the bed [...] – and she would read to me out of the university catalogues which she had sent away for" (253). Linked to her own mother by her place in the bed, the visibility of her scalp, and the coldness of the tea by her bed, Del's mother is nonetheless given the adjectives "tender," "shining," and is shown to be preoccupied with her daughter's future and with her hopes for Del's achievement of "finer and higher" aims.

8 "The first thing Freud says about the drive is, if I may put it this way, that it has no day or night, no spring or autumn, no rise and fall" (Lacan, *SXI* 165).

9 See Fink, *The Lacanian Subject* 59.

10 The monetary connotations of the American dollar bill / Bill will also be activated as the uncle buys his welcome into the home by purchasing all the sweets and treats from the local store. Del, initially pleased, comments: "But I saw now that too much really might be too much" (95).

11 Critics who have not perceived the psychological underpinnings of Del's mother's resentment toward her brother tend to view Bill as being more open to the wonder of life (Blodgett 46) and Del's mother as "lack[ing] altogether a sense of mystery and the capacity for religious experience" (Martin 65).

12 Fowler comments that this image of the "downflash" represents Del's sarcastic reevaluation of her mother (190); this position does not seem tenable when the scene is viewed in context.

"BOYS AND GIRLS"

1 For more on the act and the unconscious "choice" it constitutes, see the fascinating citation from C.S. Lewis, and Žižek's commentary on it, in the introductory paragraphs of Žižek's "The Act and Its Vicissitudes."

2 Munro scholars Blodgett, Goldman, Heble, Martin, Nischik, and Ventura, through various critical lenses, have all produced sustained readings of "Boys and Girls" that focus on the gender divide to which the title directs us: a feminist critique of patriarchy (Goldman), a structuralist analysis of gendered spaces (Ventura, "Alice Munro's 'Boys and Girls'"), a broadly poststructuralist approach (Blodgett), a social-constructivist perspective on gender (Nischik), as well as more or less intuitive readings (Martin and Heble). None of these readings of the story includes a sustained Freudian or Lacanian reading of sexual difference.

3 This is only one of the numerous instances wherein Munro's work explores the pleasure in looking. See Carrington in particular on this aspect: the index entry she provides for "voyeur" includes over twenty-five references to characters involved in deliberate, accidental, forced, or fantasized situations of voyeuristic looking.

4 "The resolution of the Oedipus complex depends upon identification with the father, or in other words, on the formation of I(O) the ego-Ideal, from traits borrowed from the father … On this point, Lacan indicates that the girl-child follows the same path as the boy. She is not, for all that, transformed into a man, but she identifies with significant traits or insignia of the father, such as 'I cough like my father does'" (Marret-Maleval 6–7).

5 Ajay Heble's reading of the story redirected my attention to this mother-daughter exchange.

6 This doubling of the father is repeated through the figure of Henry, the father's "true" hired man, as we will see further on.

7 "The sentiment of shame is occasioned … when in the exterior space of social existence, of public appearance, I suddenly appear in the flesh" ("The Object-Gaze" 178). Although Copjec is discussing the gaze in relation to shame, the embarrassment of the girl seems to me to be of the same order, the difference being one of degree.

8 Rasporich has pointed out the De Beauvoir undertones of the position of the young girl in search of self-definition (38).

9 One of the implications of this difference is outlined by Copjec in her statement that each sex will confront its fundamental sense of loss in a

different way: whereas men may feel "that the world does not measure up to some ideal, however vaguely this ideal may be conceived," women may experience dissatisfaction as "a feeling that the world lacks any legitimate ground" (*Imagine* 116). Ragland formulates this in terms of degrees of servitude to the superego: "That feminine sexuality is not all under symbolic (phallic) injunctions, means that women are less enslaved to the Other's superego dicta ... What Freud considered male superego superiority is what Lacan calls the enslavement to a master discourse logic wherein reality and language are 'measurable' as clear communications made within conscious meaning" (*From Aristotle to Lacan* 16).

10 This proposition does not negate the oedipal question developed above; rather, it is its point of knotty complexity: "The Oedipus complex is ... nothing less than the passage from the imaginary order to the symbolic order, 'the conquest of the symbolic relation as such.' The fact that the [transition] to the symbolic passes via a complex sexual dialectic means that the subject cannot have access to the symbolic order without confronting the problem of sexual difference" (*No Subject*: "Oedipus Complex").

11 The pictures in these calendars contrast with those in the kitchen of the house, which show scenes of the colonial history of Canada. These calendars have generated critical interest: see, for example, Goldman.

12 Ragland underscores this point: "Lacan's real father denotes a paradox: the production of *jouissance*, which occurs at the moment desire becomes law. The real father at the heart of the sexual masquerade points to the impossibilities or impasses in being, knowing, and speaking the truth as pure CONTRADICTION" ("Sexual Masquerade" 70).

13 My argument here differs somewhat from that of Nischik and other critics who see in this refusal "rebellion against the father" (215). This formulation seems to attribute too much intention to the act. Here, there is no attempt to undermine the father's work or his authority per se. Rather, as Žižek notes, there is a certain "madness," a temporary "eclipse, *aphanisis,* of the subject" involved in the act, whereby "the subject is annihilated and subsequently reborn" (*Enjoy* 51). In the story, the act marks this moment of the subjective transformation of the girl.

14 Like the capitalized Woman pursued by Man, Flora, once she leaves the enclosure, no longer exists, but only ex-sists as an internalized impossibility: that of existing outside the symbolic order.

15 Indeed, the girl closes the gate behind the men when they set off to capture Flora (125).

16 Flora, having escaped, becomes the feminine object outside the masculine limit; in this sense, she can also be seen as a figuration of the objet a, the partial object of the drive. But also, from the feminine perspective, Flora's flight through the gate gives metaphorical embodiment to the jouissance that is not within the symbolic field, or feminine jouissance.

17 On this point, see Soler, *What Lacan Said* 101–2. Moreover, the question of the deflation of the child, who is the narrator's early "self," leads some readers to assume that the narrator is speaking from a sterile or unfulfilling present, the origin of which the story accounts for. In my view, the story simply remains silent, or more precisely, enigmatic, about the question of what the subjective effects of the moment of assuming one's symbolic castration might be.

18 Tickling, within Munro's oeuvre, is a key image of paradoxical jouissance, an experience that readily shifts into other scenes of being "unbearably, almost exquisitely humiliated" ("Heirs of the Living Body," *Lives* 49). In her 2009 collection alone, *Too Much Happiness*, tickling scenes occur at least four times in three separate stories: "Wenlock Edge" (91), "Face" (153), and "Some Women" (170, 180).

19 For a nuanced reading of the Lacanian distinction between having or being the phallus, later reworked as having or appearing, see Žižek's "Woman Is One of the Names-of-the-Father."

20 The affirmation of the feminine position of jouissance in the sexual encounter as being that of the object of masculine desire (masculine being understood as a logical position not necessarily lined up with the biological male) is included in the table of jouissances in Lacan's *SXX*, 78.

21 This formulation may sound too centred on the really existing father who is certainly the bearer of the role in the still oedipally structured universe of "Boys and Girls," but what is at stake is the metaphorical function of the father, which may be embodied by others than the biological father. For Lacan, "any shelter in which may be established a viable, temperate relation of one sex to the other necessitates the intervention ... of that medium known as the paternal metaphor" (*SXI* 276).

22 In this sense, "only a girl" may be seen as an example of the structural defamation of women inherent in the symbolic order: "She is called woman (*on la dit-femme*) and defamed (*diffâme*)" (Lacan, *SXX* 85). She is defamed "because one cannot say her with the words of phallic jouissance ... What is important here is that this ability to encompass her in words is also impossible for her" (Soler, *What Lacan Said* 104).

23 Indeed, Ragland affirms that symbolic castration includes "a 'no' to being All One sex, an androgyn" (*Logic of Sexuation* 6).

24 His sexuation will indeed fix him within this fantasy of phallic oneness, making of it his "fixion." See Soler, *What Lacan Said* 219–20, on this neologism of Lacan's; the implications of the term are also developed in the final chapter of this volume.

25 See Freud's "The Antithetical Meanings of Primal Words."

"ESKIMO"

1 A few examples are: plane, "Eskimo"; train, "Too Much Happiness" (*Too Much*) and "A Queer Streak" (*Progress*); truck, "Baptizing" (*Lives*); bus, "Wild Swans" (*The Beggar Maid*) and "Bardon Bus" (*The Moons*); car, "Simon's Luck" (*The Beggar Maid*) and "Miles City, Montana" (*Progress*); boat, "The View from Castle Rock" (*The View*); horseback, "The Albanian Virgin" (*Open Secrets*); motorcycle, "Vandals" (*Open Secrets*); roaming the streets of the town on foot, "Lives of Girls and Women" (*Lives*).

2 In relation to the plane in "Eskimo," Rasporich sees Mary Jo as "trapped within the womblike machine" (157). Although the streamlined vessel hurtling through the air might as easily be seen as a phallic object, and the recourse to organic metaphors does not, in itself, clarify matters, there is pertinence in this analogy to the extent that the womb is associated with the maternal, which will indeed be a significant element in the story's underpinning.

An earlier story, "Wild Swans" (*The Beggar Maid*), gives shape to this strain in Munro's writing, where travelling is transportation: being moved, or carried away. Riding a bus, in the random presence of a nameless older male stranger, a "minister" sitting next to her, the young protagonist on her first solo voyage away from home is led, by the roaming hand and fingers of her intrusive neighbour, to her initiatory experience of orgasmic jouissance expressed in a metaphorical issuing forth of wild swans: "You could have had such a flock of birds, wild swans, even, wakened under one big dome together, exploding from it, taking to the sky" (65). This moment corresponds to the train's coming into view of the erotically charged "gates and towers of the Exhibition Grounds," signalling the arrival at her destination. The distancing effect of the metaphorical representation of jouissance keeps the girl (and the reader) at one remove from the immediacy of the experience, which is set within a clearly signposted fantasy-type scenario, and thereby removed from danger (although the *threat* of danger is intimated by Rose's stepmother, Flo).

3 Maisonnat's article points to all of the main Lacanian questions the story raises – desire, drive, jouissance. However, it mobilizes these concepts in a way that differs entirely from the reading I propose here, linking them, in spite of the reference to the real in the article's title, to the *symbolic* coordinates of Mary Jo's life (her social position in terms of class and gender), rather than to the shock of the real that subtends the story. Other critics have tended to misconstrue the story's opacity and are wont to dismiss its complexity with such summations as "Divining her situation on her vacation trip to Tahiti, Mary Jo begins to go a little crazy" (Rasporich 84); or "[The] female protagonist senses, or imagines, a psychic kinship with a young Eskimo girl she tries to befriend on an airplane flight, but their encounter comes to nothing and the story dissolves in a self-consciously symbolic dream" (Oates). The inner complexity and resonant imagery of "Eskimo" are completely missed here.

4 The formulation "may be seen as someone trying to get hold of the girl for her own purposes," in the context of the otherness of "Eskimo," may raise questions about Mary Jo's attitude; is there a parallel to be made with a colonialist outlook and the objectification of the other defined as culturally inferior? If this possibility is inscribed in the story, it is not part of Mary Jo's character construction per se; on the contrary, through the passive structure "may be seen as," a cultural taboo is evoked from which Mary Jo wishes to distance herself. What strikes me here is Mary Jo's sense of "being seen," and possibly judged, by the other travellers.

5 The French *heur* – originally signifying fate or destiny in a neutral sense – to which *bon* or *mal* may be appended, gives us the sense of a chance encounter, for good or for ill.

6 This notion of the fundamental fantasy has also been dealt with in chapter 1, on "Royal Beatings."

7 Lacan notes the "perverse" aspect – that which takes the other as the object of one's jouissance – in male fantasy, but distinguishes perversion in neurotic fantasy from a perverse psychic structure: "Neurosis consists in dreaming, not perverse acts. Neurotics have none of the characteristics of perverts. They simply dream of being perverts, which is quite natural, for how else could they attain their partner?" (*SXX* 87).

8 "The human being, because he is a speaking being, carries within him the trauma of language. Speech, in effect, cannot say everything. There is a hole

[*un trou*] in the real that nothing can fill. This is what Lacan noted down in his formulation 'There is no sexual relation.' That creates a *troumatisme* (*SXXI*, 17 February 1974). This neologism offers the advantage of being meaningful. It refers to the hole in language which founds trauma. From this results the subjective suffering that the subject complains of" (Attié).

9 Another of Munro's stories, "Before the Change" (*The Love of*), has structural similarities to "Eskimo" and includes this nexus of "washroom, rust, doll." Like "Eskimo," it involves a dedicated doctor, who in this case performs illegal abortions. There is a question of a possible love relationship with his assistant ("For love, then" 338), but the story is narrated through his daughter's voice, and her focus returns insistently to the bathroom. First, she notices "cracks like brown hairs in the downstairs washbasin and a disconcerting spot of rust in the toilet" (298). This proleptic disconcerting rust marks the place where she, standing in for the absent assistant, goes to discard the uterine waste, the "plops of wine jelly, and blood, and somewhere in there the fetus." The undesired child is brought into the sphere of the doll-like through a comparison: "Like a bauble in the cereal box or the prize in the popcorn. A tiny plastic doll as negligible as a fingernail" (321), and again, as a condensed image of the unwanted child-doll-love – "A mud doll with hollow eye sockets" (339) – when she evokes her own lost love relationship.

10 Redekop points out that the signifier "count" may be associated with Khan, counting his purported harem.

11 Blue was the colour of the feminine in the West until the 1960s when toy manufacturers decided otherwise.

"TOO MUCH HAPPINESS"

1 There are variants on the spelling of her name: Sofia, Sophie, and the alternate first name Sonya; Kovalevsky is sometimes written Kowalevski or Kowalevsky. I am following Munro's choice of spelling here.

2 "Another way of saying this is that without the constitutive illusion of the phallic exception as limit, the *symbolic becomes,* in a sense, *real*" (Barnard, "Tongues of Angels" 179).

3 Brousse adds that these metonymic objects of the feminine may be understood as belonging to the category of the phallus. The phallus is understood here as "the signifier that comes into function to organize desire in both sexes and which, in the form of maternal objects transmitted from

mother to daughter … is linked to the orientation of desire" ("Qu'est-ce qu'une femme?").

4 Another such illumination of the sky will be seen in the next chapter, on "Tell Me Yes or No."

5 See Barnard, "Tongues of Angels" 179–85 on this aspect of Lacan's *SXX*.

"TELL ME YES OR NO"

1 The present and past tenses will serve as markers throughout the intertwined narratives: the past tense signals the reminiscence of their "falling in love," and the present tense the unreal present of the death fantasy. A misprint in later editions of the story has posed problems for some critical attempts to sort out the time frame: where the original text reads "Would you like to know how I am informed of your death," inscribing the verbal notion "be informed" in the present tense and therefore within the fantasy framework, the New American Library of Canada edition puts this in the past tense, written as "how I was informed," giving the impression that the news of the lover's death belongs to a historical past.

2 But the lack of determination of the nominal phrase also leaves open questions: *what exactly* was exaggerated, the *love*, or the *then*, and was it still an exaggeration later? Would it be "now"?

3 "In love, as in desire, something of the primordial situation of the child is played out, the child, who, through birth, is thrown into the spider's web of libidinal investments, and who will grow up knowing that he or she is the centre of a certain number of libidinal investments of others, but who will never know *precisely what* others see in him" (Hoornaert). The capture of the child in the libidinal investments of its Other is related to the presubjective origins of the emerging subject, the "dark stain" that is the leftover of the "passionate attachment" to the primary Other, as well as to the possibility of the nonexistence of this bond – this is indeed what the beating fantasy seen in relation to my analysis of "Royal Beatings" brought out. Following Baas's reading of Žižek, "[If] it is true that without this passionate attachment the child does not exist, it is nevertheless this potential nonexistence which makes the very being of the child: to be attached to the Other is to be this nothing that you would be if the attachment did not exist. And this being that is nothing, is what the Thing is."

4 Generally speaking, this "someone" doesn't want it since their desire, as distinct from their love, is for the objet a, or for something that promises, precisely, to fill their own lack.

5 Moreover, to the extent that it looks for identification between two subjects, looks for similarity rather than difference, it is *hommosexual*, a spelling that points to several directions of Lacan's work on sexuality: masculine jouissance targets the objet a (which belongs in the last instance to the one who pursues it, since it is the *cause* of their desire) and not the Otherness of the other. To that extent, love, which also targets identification, forecloses the other's Otherness.

6 See my analysis of "Boys and Girls" in this volume.

7 The etymological root of "happiness" is *hap:* the chance, luck or fortune, *either good or bad*, that befalls someone; happiness just "*hap*"pens.

8 In order to satisfy his needs the infant must articulate them in language; in other words, the infant must articulate his needs in a "demand." However, in doing so, something else is introduced that causes a split between need and demand, in that every demand is not only an articulation of need but also an (unconditional) demand for love. Now, although the other to whom the demand is addressed (in the first instance, the mother) can and may supply the object that satisfies the infant's need, she is never in a position to answer the demand for love unconditionally because she, too, is divided. The result of this split between need and demand is an insatiable leftover, which is desire itself (*No Subject*: "Need").

9 The French form of "*ne cesse* pas de s'écrire" makes apparent the etymology of "necessary."

10 Ajay Heble questions this intermixing of reality and "construct" in "Tell Me Yes or No," seeing its uncertainty effect as "something of her [Munro's] personal signature" (82).

11 "The riddle, or enigma, is a basic speech-form – a minimal enunciation (*énonciation*) – which compels the one to whom it is addressed to respond in the form of a statement (*énoncé*). The hysteric's enunciation is injunctive: 'Tell me!'" (Wajcman).

12 Letters in Munro's stories revive lost loves, "I dreamed that X wrote me a letter" ("Bardon Bus," *The Moons* 114), provide epilogues to or revisions of past lives ("Friend of My Youth," *Friend of*; "Wilderness Station," *Open Secrets*), or set in motion new destinies ("Hateship, Friendship, Courtship, Loveship, Marriage," *Hateship, Friendship*).

13 This section owes much to the discussion of the love letter in Jean Allouch's *L'amour Lacan,* notably chapter 16, "L'amour écrit, il ne rature pas" (Love writes, but does not engrave).

14 Cf. Margaret Atwood's short story "The Grave of the Famous Poet," which deals with similar questions of going through the end of love and

questioning what comes after the end. The female narrator says, early in the story, "I have the map," following which a similar quest and misalignment of desires, in a mood of anxiety, fills the space of love's questions. See Murray, "The End of the World."

15 The narrator's enthrallment is structurally similar to the scene in Freud's case study on hysteria, the case of Dora: Lacan comments on Dora's two-hour contemplation of the Sistine Madonna in Dresden, linking the portrait of the virgin to Frau K., her father's mistress. In contemplating the figure, Dora is understood to be trying to pierce the mystery of desire, or more precisely, what the embodied knowledge of the Woman, the one "who knows how to sustain the desire of the idealised father" might be (*SXVII,* 11 February 1970).

16 Translation slightly modified.

17 Cf. Lacan, *SX*, 26 March 1963, and *SXX* 10.

18 For Don Juan, the magical number is one thousand and three – at least for his Spanish conquests.

19 "It is in the opaque place of jouissance of the Other, of the Other insofar as woman, if she existed, could be it, that the Supreme Being is situated – this Supreme Being that is manifestly mythical in Aristotle's work, this unmoving sphere from which all movements stem, whatever they may be: changes, generations, motions, translations, increases, etc." (Lacan, *SXX* 82–3).

20 The expression is inferred from Copjec's "The Inheritance of Potentiality."

21 This is stated quite explicitly in another story, "Bardon Bus": "There is a limit to the amount of misery and disarray you will put up with, for love, just as there is a limit to the amount of mess you can stand around a house. You can't know the limit beforehand, but you will know when you've reached it. I believe this" (127).

22 For the association between litter and the letter see Lacan's "Joyce le symptôme."

23 "A woman is a symptom of a man, in the sense that a woman can only ever enter the psychic economy of men as a fantasy object (a), the cause of their desire" (*No Subject*: "Woman").

24 This passage is also reminiscent of an earlier part of the story where she *did* read stories: case histories of the suffering of women in love, with whom she could identify, and from whom she could take comfort, "because it is a comfort to discover that one's own case holds no particular agony, only some shopworn recognizable pain" (117).

25 Unconscious knowledge is "impossible to master, it is 'without a master.' The defeat of Descartes: the subject of psychoanalysis is perhaps the Cartesian subject of science, but the knowledge of the unconscious is not the knowledge of science" (Soler, *Lacan* ch. 5).

EPILOGUE

1 Soler refers in this section to the debates around the status of the author and, in particular, to Roland Barthes's 1967 essay, "The Death of the Author," and to Foucault's "reply" to Barthes in his 1969 lecture, "What Is an Author?" wherein "he emphasized [the extent to which] this dimension of the One of the author was ineradicable" (ch. 1). Lacan, as Soler notes, attended Foucault's lecture.

2 I have used this term in "For the Love of a Fish" to pick up on Lacan's metaphor in "Lituraterre," where the presymbolic letter is metaphorically seen to have a gullying effect, simultaneously crossing out and marking a place (*raturer*).

3 Part of the development here is adapted from my article, "Honte et Humiliation." Note also the detailed study of the question of humiliation in Carrington.

4 See also Francesconi (5) for a reading of the linoleum in this story.

Works Cited

Adams, Parveen. "Father, Can't You See I'm Filming?" Copjec, *Supposing the Subject* 185–200.

Albertazzi, Silvia. "A Comparative Essay on the Sociology of Literature: Alice Munro's Unconsummated Relationships." *Journal of the Short Story in English* 55 (2010): 37–53.

Allouch, Jean. *L'amour Lacan*. Paris: Epel, 2009.

Attié, Joseph. "Traumatisme et savoir." *Ecole de la Cause Freudienne.* Web. 10 July 2014.

Atwood, Margaret. "The Grave of the Famous Poet." *Dancing Girls and Other Stories.* (1977). New York: Anchor Books, 1998.

– *Surfacing*. (1972). London: Virago, 1979.

Baas, B. "Les pulsions III. 5 Échanges dialogués. Séminaire de J.R. Freymann." *Fedepsy.* Web. 21 July 2014.

Badiou, Alain. *In Praise of Love*. Interview with Nicolas Truong. Trans. Peter Bush. London: Serpent's Tail, 2012.

Barnard, Suzanne. "Tongues of Angels: Feminine Structure and Other Jouissance." Barnard and Fink 171–85.

Barnard, Suzanne, and Bruce Fink, eds. *Reading Seminar XX: Lacan's Major Work on Love, Knowledge, and Feminine Sexuality*. New York: SUNY, 2002.

Barthes, Roland. "The Death of the Author" (1967). *Ubuweb Papers.* PDF file. Trans. Richard Howard. Web. 22 July 2014.

– "Fragments d'un discours amoureux." *Œuvres complètes*. Tome 5. 1977–1980. Paris: Seuil, 2002.

Beer, Janet. "Short Fiction with Attitude: The Lives of Boys and Men in the Lives of Girls and Women." *Yearbook of English Studies* 31 (2001): 125–32.

Bergeron, Danielle. "Femininity." *American Journal of Semiotics* 8.4 (1981): 5–15.

Bettelheim, Bruno. *The Uses of Enchantment.* London: Penguin, 1975.

Blodgett, E.D. *Alice Munro*. Boston: Twayne, 1988.

Brousse, Marie-Hélène. "Sexual Position and the End of Analysis." Voruz and Wolf 251–8.

– "Qu'est-ce qu'une femme?" *Sixième Conférence du Pont Freudien.* 18 February 2000. Web. 20 June 2015.

Canellopoulos, Lissy. "The Bodily Event, *Jouissance* and the (Post)Modern Subject." *Recherches en Psychanalyse*. Trans. Kristina Valendinova. 10 (2010). Web. 30 July 2014.

Carrington, Ildikó de Papp. *Controlling the Uncontrollable*. Dekalb: North Illinois University Press, 1989.

Copjec, Joan. *Imagine There's No Woman: Ethics and Sublimation.* MIT Press, 2004.

– "The Inheritance of Potentiality." Interview with Jennifer Murray. *E-rea* 12.1. Fall 2014. Web. 14 December 2014.

– "The Object-Gaze: Shame, Hejab, Cinema." *Filzofski Vestnik* (2006): 163–83. Web. June 2013.

– *Read My Desire: Lacan against the Historicists*. Cambridge: MIT Press, 1995.

– ed. *Supposing the Subject.* London: Verso, 1994.

Corelli, Richard J. "Dreams and Symbols." Web. 12 December 2009.

Dawkins, Laura. "'Something You Have Always Known Was There': Figures of Death in Alice Munro's 'Images' and 'The Peace of Utrecht.'" *The Inside of a Shell: Alice Munro's* Dance of the Happy Shades. Ed. Vanessa Guignery. Newcastle upon Tyne: Cambridge Scholars Publishing, 2015. 144–55.

Dockstader, Nels. "Spinoza's Epistemology." *Internet Encyclopedia of Philosophy*. 13 September 2009. Web. 2 February 2012.

Ferri, Laura. "Mothers and Other Secrets." *Open Letter* 11.9/12.1 (2004): 137–50.

Fink, Bruce. *A Clinical Introduction to Lacanian Psychoanalysis: Theory and Technique.* Cambridge: Harvard University Press, 1997.

– *Lacan to the Letter*. Minneapolis: University of Minnesota Press, 2004.

– *The Lacanian Subject: Between Language and Jouissance*. Princeton: Princeton University Press, 1995.

Fiumanò, Marisa. "L'amour c'est donner ce qu'on n'a pas." *Association Lacanienne Internationale*. Web. 18 July 2013.

Foucault, Michel. "What Is an Author?" (1969). *Wiki.brown.edu*. PDF Trans. Josué V. Harari. Web. 22 July 2014.

Fowler, Rowena. "The Art of Alice Munro: The Beggar Maid and Lives of Girls and Women." *Critique* 25.4 (1984): 189–98. Web. 18 July 2008.

Francesconi, Sabrina. "Alice Munro and the Poetics of the Linoleum." *The Inside of a Shell: Alice Munro's* Dance of the Happy Shades. Ed. Vanessa Guignery. Newcastle upon Tyne: Cambridge Scholars Publishing, 2015. 86–97.

Freud, Sigmund. "A Child Is Being Beaten: A Contribution to the Study of the Origin of Sexual Perversions." 1919. *Penguin Freud Library 10: On Psychopathology.* Ed. Angela Richards. Trans. James Strachey. London: Penguin, 1979. 159–93.

– "The Antithetical Meanings of Primal Words." 1910. *Standard Edition 11*. London: Hogarth, 1964. 153–61.

– *Civilization and Its Discontents*. 1929. Ed. James Strachey. Trans. Joan Rivière. London: Hogarth Press, 1973.

– "On Narcissism: An Introduction." 1914. *On Metapsychology: The Theory of Psychoanalysis*. Ed. Angela Richards. Trans. James Strachey. Harmondsworth: Penguin, 1984. 59–97.

– "Psychoanalytic Notes on an Autobiographical Account of a Case of Paranoia (Schreber)." 1910. *Penguin Freud Library 9: Case Histories II.* Ed. Angela Richards. London: Penguin Books, 1979. 131–223.

– "Repression." 1915. *Penguin Freud Library 9:* On *Metapsychology: The Theory of Psychoanalysis*. Ed. Angela Richards. Trans. James Strachey. Harmondsworth: Penguin, 1984. 145–58.

– *Totem and Taboo: Resemblances between the Psychic Lives of Savages and Neurotics*. 1919. Project Gutenberg: e-book, 28 October 2012. Web.

Goldman, Marlene. "Penning in the Bodies: The Construction of Gendered Subjects in Alice Munro's 'Boys and Girls.'" *Studies in Canadian Literature* 15.1 (1990): 62–75. Web. 28 December 2009.

Guéguen, Pierre-Gilles. "Discretion of the Analyst." Voruz and Wolf 10–24.

Halpern, Richard. "Creation: Lacan in Kansas." *Journal for Religious and Cultural Theory* 2.1 (2001). Web. 8 October 2014.

Heble, Ajay. *The Tumble of Reason: Alice Munro's Discourse of Absence*. Toronto: University of Toronto Press, 1994.

Heller, Deborah. "Getting Loose: Women and Narration in Alice Munro's Friend of My Youth." Thacker, *The Rest of the Story* 60–80.

Hoornaert, Geert. "L'amour." *Cripsablog*. Web. 4 December 2013.

Howells, Coral Ann. *Alice Munro*. Manchester: Manchester University Press, 1998.

Lacan, Jacques. *Autres Écrits.* Paris: Editions du Seuil, 2001.

"Joyce le symptôme." 565–70.

"Lituraterre." 11–20.

– *Ecrits.* 1966. Trans. Bruce Fink. New York: Norton, 2006.

"Remarks on Daniel Lagache's Presentation." 543–74.

"Seminar on the Purloined Letter." 6–48.

– *The Seminars of Jacques Lacan.*

Seminar I: Freud's Papers on Technique, 1953–1954. Ed. Jacques-Alain Miller. Trans. John Forrester. New York: Norton, 2013.

Seminar VII: The Ethics of Psychoanalysis, 1959–1960. Ed. Jacques-Alain Miller. Trans. Dennis Porter. London: Routledge, 1992.

Seminar X: Anxiety, 1962–1963. Unofficial translation, Cormac Gallagher. *LacaninIreland.* Web. 20 June 2014.

Seminar XI: The Four Fundamental Concepts of Psycho-Analysis, 1964. Ed. Jacques-Alain Miller. Trans. Alan Sheridan. London: Penguin, 1977.

Seminar XVII: The Other Side of Psychoanalysis, 1969–1970. Unofficial translation, Cormac Gallagher. *LacaninIreland.* Web. 19 June 2014.

Seminaire XVIII: D'un discours qui ne serait pas du semblant: 1970–1971 (Unpublished). *Staferla.* Web. 14 February 2010.

Seminar XX: On Feminine Sexuality: The Limits of Love and Knowledge, 1972–1973: Encore. Ed. Jacques-Alain Miller. Trans. Bruce Fink. New York: Norton, 1999.

Seminar XXI: Les Non-dupes errent, 1973–1974. (Unpublished). *Staferla.* Web.

Seminar XXIII: Le Sinthome, 1975–1976. (Unpublished). *Staferla.* Web.

– *Television.* Lacan interviewed by Jacques-Alain Miller. 1973. Ed. Joan Copjec. Trans. Denis Hollier, Rosalind Krauss, Annette Michelson. New York: Norton, 1990.

Leader, Darian. "Beating Fantasies and Sexuality." Salecl, *Sexuation* 106–30.

MacCannell, Juliet Flower. "Fascism and the Voice of Conscience." *The Hysteric's Guide to the Future Female Subject.* Minneapolis: University of Minnesota Press, 2000.

MacDonald, Rae McCarthy. "Structure and Detail in Lives of Girls and Women." *Studies in Canadian Literature* 3 (1978). Web. 23 December 2009.

MacKendrick, Louis K., ed. *Probable Fictions: Alice Munro's Narrative Acts.* Toronto: ECW Press, 1983.

Maisonnat, Claude. "'Eskimo' or an Encounter with the Real of Feminine Desire." *Journal of the Short Story in English* 55 (2010): 71–82.

Marret-Maleval, Sophie. "Le pas-tout sans le ravage." *Lacan-université.fr.* Web. 15 October 2012.

Martin, W.R. "Chapter 4: Lives of Girls and Women." *Paradox and Parallel.* Edmonton: University of Alberta Press, 1987. 58–76.

McCaig, JoAnn. *Reading in: Alice Munro's Archives.* Waterloo: Wilfrid Laurier University Press, 2002.

McCulloch, Jeanne, and Mona Simpson. "Alice Munro: The Art of Fiction, No. 137." *The Paris Review Interviews* 131 (Summer 1994). Web. 28 December 2009.

Michaux, Ginette. *De Sophocle à Proust, de Nerval à Boulgakov: essai de psychanalyse lacanienne.* Ramonville-Saint-Agne: Eres, 2008.

Miller, Jacques-Alain. "Σ(x)." *The Symptom.* Trans. Daniel Collins. 5 (2004). Web. 7 August 2013.

– "On Love." Interview with Hanna Waar. *Psychologies Magazine* 278. October 2008. Trans. Adrian Price. *Lacan.com.* Web. 14 February 2014.

– "Reading a Symptom." Transcript of "*Presentation of the Theme for the Tenth Congress of the NLS.*" 3 Apr. 2011. Trans. Adrian Price. *The Symptom / Lacan.com.* Web. 5 February 2012.

– "The Sinthome: A Mixture of Symptom and Fantasy." Voruz and Wolf 55–72.

Morel, Genevieve. "Feminine Conditions of Jouissance." Barnard and Fink 77–92.

Munro, Alice. *The Beggar Maid.* 1977. Originally published as *Who Do You Think You Are?* New York: Vintage, 1991.

"Royal Beatings." 3–24.

"Simon's Luck." 156–77.

"Wild Swans." 57–67.

– *Dance of the Happy Shades.* 1974. London: Vintage, 2000.

"Boys and Girls." 111–27.

"Dance of the Happy Shades." 211–24.

"Images." 30–43.

"The Peace of Utrecht." 190–210.

"Sunday Afternoon." 161–71.
"The Time of Death." 89–99.
"Walker Brothers Cowboy." 1–18.
– *Friend of My Youth.* Toronto: Penguin, 1990.
"Friend of My Youth." 3–26.
– *Hateship, Friendship, Courtship, Loveship, Marriage.* London: Vintage, 2001.
"Hateship, Friendship, Courtship, Loveship, Marriage." 3–54.
"Post and Beam." 188–218.
– *Lives of Girls and Women.* 1971. New York: Vintage, 2001.
"Baptizing." 195–264.
"Epilogue: The Photographer." 265–77.
"Heirs of the Living Body." 33–71.
"Lives of Girls and Women." 157–94.
"Princess Ida." 72–101.
– *The Love of a Good Woman.* 1998. Toronto: Penguin, 1999.
"Before the Change." 295–339.
"Cortes Island." 134–67.
"The Love of a Good Woman." 1–89.
– *The Moons of Jupiter.* 1982. London: Vintage, 2004.
"Accident." 77–109.
"Bardon Bus." 110–28.
"Dulse." 36–59.
"Introduction." xiii–xvi.
"The Turkey Season." 60–76.
– *Open Secrets.* New York: Vintage, 1995.
"The Albanian Virgin." 81–128.
"Vandals." 261–94.
"A Wilderness Station." 190–225.
– *The Progress of Love.* Toronto: Penguin, 1986.
"Circle of Prayer." 346–73.
"Eskimo." 257–82.
"Fits." 143–78.
"Miles City, Montana." 113–42.
"The Progress of Love." 3–41.
"A Queer Streak." 283–345.
– *Something I've Been Meaning to Tell You.* Toronto: McGraw-Hill Ryerson, 1974.

"Tell Me Yes or No." 106–24.
– *Something I've Been Meaning to Tell You*. Scarborough: The New American Library of Canada, 1975.
"The Ottawa Valley." 182–97.
– *Too Much Happiness*. New York: Alfred A. Knopf, 2009.
"Face." 140–64.
"Some Women." 165–88.
"Too Much Happiness." 247–304.
"Wenlock Edge." 64–94.
– *The View from Castle Rock*. London: Vintage, 2007.
"Fathers." 173–96.
"The View from Castle Rock." 27–87.
"What Do You Want to Know For?" 316–40.
"The Wilds of Morris Township." 111–26.
"Working for a Living." 127–70.
– "What Is Real?" *Making It New: Contemporary Canadian Stories*. Ed. John Metcalf. Auckland: Methuen, 1982. 223–6.

Murray, Jennifer. "'The End of the World': Desire and Desolation in Margaret Atwood's 'The Grave of the Famous Poet.'" *Journal of the Short Story in English* 31 (1998): 71–79.

– "For the Love of a Fish: A Lacanian Reading of Margaret Atwood's *Surfacing*." *Literature, Interpretation, Theory* 26.1 (Winter 2015): 1–21. Online. 13 February 2015.

– "Honte et Humiliation: reconfigurations d'une écriture de soi chez Alice Munro." *Transmission des savoirs et reconfigurations des identités*. Laurence Dahan-Gaida, ed. *e-CRIT3224* 2 (2011): 71–81. Web. 15 April 2011.

Murray, Jennifer, and Lee Garner. "From Participant to Observer: Theatricality as Distantiation in Alice Munro's 'Lives of Girls and Women' and 'Royal Beatings.'" *Journal of the Short Story in English* 51 (2008): 149–58. *Revues.org*. Web.

Nischik, Reingard. *The Canadian Short Story: Interpretations*. Rochester: Camden House, 2007.

No Subject: An Encyclopedia of Lacanian Psychoanalysis. Web. 9 October 2014.

Oates, Joyce Carol. "Characters Dangerously Like Us." *New York Times Review of Books*. 14 September 1986. Web. 28 May 2012.

Pickmann, Claude-Noële. "L'hystérique et le ravage." *Actualité de l'hystérie*. Ed. André Michels. Ramonville Saint-Agne: Erès, 2001. 159–89.

Rabaté, Jean-Michel, ed. *The Cambridge Companion to Lacan.* Cambridge: Cambridge University Press, 2003.

– *Jacques Lacan: Psychoanalysis and the Subject of Literature.* New York: Palgrave, 2001.

– "Psychoanalysis Applicable and Inapplicable: The Case of Literature." *The Literary Lacan: From Literature to Lituraterre and Beyond.* Ed. Santanu Biswas. London: Seagull, 2012. 51–85.

Ragland, Ellie. *The Logic of Sexuation: From Aristotle to Lacan.* Albany: SUNY Press, 2004.

– "The Sexual Masquerade: A Lacanian Theory of Sexual Difference." Ragland-Sullivan and Bracher 49–80.

– "The Woman Not Seen." *European Journal of Psychoanalysis* 20.1 (2001). Web. 20 June 2014.

Ragland-Sullivan, Ellie, and Mark Bracher, eds. *Lacan and the Subject of Language.* New York: Routledge, 1991.

Rasporich, Beverly. *Dance of the Sexes: Art and Gender in the Fiction of Alice Munro.* Edmonton: University of Alberta Press, 1990.

Redekop, Magdalene. *Mothers and Other Clowns: The Stories of Alice Munro.* London: Routledge, 1992.

Salecl, Renata. "Love Anxieties." Barnard and Fink 93–97.

– ed. *Sexuation.* Durham: Duke University Press, 2000.

Sartre, Jean-Paul. *Being and Nothingness.* Trans. Hazel Barnes. New York: Washington Square Press, 1992.

Sharpe, Matthew. "Jacques Lacan." *Internet Encyclopedia of Philosophy.* Web. 13 October 2012.

Soler, Colette. *Lacan: The Unconscious Reinvented.* 2014. Originally published as *Lacan, L'inconscient Réinventé.* Presses Universitaires de France, 2009. Kindle.

– "Literature as Symptom." Ragland-Sullivan and Bracher 213–19.

– "The Paradoxes of the Symptom in Psychoanalysis." Rabaté, *The Cambridge Companion to Lacan* 86–101.

– "Some Remarks on the Love Letter." Transcript from Freudian Field Seminar London in July 1993. Web. 3 November 2013.

– *What Lacan Said about Women.* Trans. John Holland. New York: Other Press, 2003.

Stevens, Alexandre. "Love and Sex beyond Identifications." Voruz and Wolf 211–21.

Struthers, J.M. (Tim). "The Real Material: An Interview with Alice Munro." MacKendrick 5–36.

Tausky, Thomas E. "Biocritical Essay." University of Calgary, Special Collections: Munro, Alice. 1986. Web. 8 April 2011.

Thacker, Robert. *Alice Munro: Writing Her Lives*. Toronto: McClelland & Stewart, 2005.

– "'Clear Jelly': Alice Munro's Narrative Dialectics." *Probable Fictions: Alice Munro's Narrative Acts*. Ed. Louis K. MacKendrick. Toronto: ECW Press, 1983. 37–60.

– "Introduction: Alice Munro, Writing 'Home': 'Seeing This Trickle in Time.'" *The Rest of the Story*. 1–20.

– ed. *The Rest of the Story: Critical Essays on Alice Munro*. Toronto: ECW Press, 1999.

Ventura, Héliane. "Alice Munro's 'Boys and Girls': Mapping out Boundaries." *Commonwealth Essays and Studies* 15.1 (1992): 80–7.

– "The Setting Up of Unsettlement in Alice Munro's 'Tell Me Yes or No.'" *Postmodern Fiction in Canada*. Ed. Theo D'haen and Hans Bertens. Amsterdam: Rodopi, 1992. 105–23.

Verhaeghe, Paul. "Lacan's Answer to the Classical Mind / Body Deadlock." Barnard and Fink 109–39.

Verhaeghe, Paul, and Frédéric Declercq. "Lacan's Analytic Goal: Le sinthome or the Feminine Way." *Re-Inventing the Symptom: Essays on the Final Lacan*. Ed. Luke Thurston. New York: Other Press, 2002. 59–82.

Voruz, Véronique. "A Lacanian Reading of Dora." Voruz and Wolf 158–9.

Voruz, Véronique, and Bogdan Wolf. *The Later Lacan: An Introduction*. Albany: SUNY Press, 2007.

Wajcman, Gérard. "The Hysteric's Discourse." *The Symptom* 4 (Spring 2003). Web. 14 August 2014.

Žižek, Slavoj. "The Act and Its Vicissitudes." *The Symptom* 6 (2005). Web. 2 June 2011.

– *Enjoy Your Symptom: Jacques Lacan in Hollywood and Out*. New York: Routledge, 1992.

– *How to Read Lacan*. London: Granta Books, 2006.

– "Is It Possible to Traverse the Fantasy in Cyberspace?" *The Žižek Reader*. Eds. Elizabeth Wright and Edmond Wright. Oxford: Blackwell, 1999. 102–24.

– "Is There a Cause of the Subject?" Copjec, *Supposing the Subject* 85–105.

– *The Sublime Object of Ideology*. London: Verso, 1989.
– "The Truth Arises from Misrecognition." Ragland-Sullivan and Bracher 188–212.
– "Woman Is One of the Names-of-the-Father, or How Not to Misread Lacan's Formulas of Sexuation." *Lacanian Ink* 10 (1995). Web. 12 April 2011.

Index